Embracing the Darkness and the Light...

Embracing the Darkness
and the Light...

By
Fritz O'Skennick

ISBN 978-1-4478-3279-9

Dedicated to Shaun & Romana...

With special thanks to Jayde Antonin, William Ford & Adam Foreman for all their help and support with all my projects and wacky schemes...

Congratulations and thank you also to Sarah & Pete for bringing my lovely niece, Olivia Rose into the world and finally making me an uncle... xxx

Contents...

<u>Foreword</u>

"Embracing the Darkness and the Light" is a startling collection of new poetry and prose from dark writer and poet, **Fritz O'Skennick.** This collection features a number of touching tributes and dedications to his idols, his children and friends interspersed with powerful messages to the future and lessons to humanity. This is quickly followed by a new chapter of his chilling and ever popular 'Gothic Tales'. Next we move on to a chapter of humorous poetry as expressed in his outrageous and unique style. Finally, the book finishes up with a chapter of deep, powerful verses of self exploration and inner thoughts that many can relate too.

   Fritz O'Skennick is an accomplished creative artist and writer with many strings to his bow. As a singer/songwriter, poet, novelist, playwright/actor & performer, he has enjoyed varying successes with a number of his projects.

   Previously published, some of his lighter work has appeared in various anthologies with other poets as produced by United Press.

   His solo debut into literary publication was **"Touching the Darkness"** a highly anticipated anthology of his dark poetry that concentrates solely on his darker work that many have come to enjoy via Allpoetry.com and via performances throughout Wales and parts of England.

His second book **"Fear the Reaper"** is a unique, intense, first-person psychological crime thriller that tells a schizophrenic tale of love, loss, revenge and madness.

This was quickly followed by his third book **"The Darkness Verses The Light"** which is a mixed genre collection of poetry, prose and short stories.

His fourth book **"Who is John Doe?"** is a unique supernatural drama based on his popular stage show of the same name.

His fifth book **"Of Darkness and Light"** is a collection of poetry and prose, featuring new work and also many outstanding collaborative works with fellow poets from all over the World, including a collaboration that features no less than 40 poets in 1 poem as orchestrated and edited by Fritz.

His sixth book **"Dark Confessions"** is an intense serial killer novella and concentrates on the darker nature of man, exploring the facets and mind states of murder, revenge and the lengths we'd go to in the name of love, honor and redemption...

His seventh book **"Gothic Tales"** is a definitive collection of his ever popular supernatural poetry, featuring vampires, werewolves, ghost stories, murder, immortality and various other themes based in science fiction and fantasy.

His eighth book **"Schizophrenic Lullabies"** is an insightful and revealing collection of dark poetry themed in the realms of mental illness.

His debut album **"UNspokeN"** (music) was released on Petrified Records in 2005 amidst a string of impressive reviews and radio play all over the world.

Playwright and acting credits include **"It could Happen to You"** and **"Who is John Doe?"** as produced by the former theatre company "Progress Cymru".

He is presently working on a second album of his music **"UNbrokeN",** his new book **"Just the Lyrics"** and writing his epic new trilogy of sci-fi books **"Temporal Medium"**.

For further details of his poetry go to
http://allpoetry.com/Fritz%20O%20skennick

For further details of his music go to
http://www.myspace.com/fracturedpersona

For further details of his performance poetry go to
http://www.myspace.com/fritzo39skennick

Dedications & Messages...

Working Class Hero: *A Journey in the life*

1940, Liverpool
as bombs fell all around,
Julia, sweet Julia,
your path in life is bound.
You bring an icon to a world,
who dares to say 'No more'
Its time we all 'Give peace a chance'
And all say no to war...

But your life was cut so short,
knocked down by drunken cop,
so lost the child you left behind,
was destined for the top.
'Please watch over little John,
I know he'll make you proud,
bestowed to you, his Aunt Mimi,
he's sure to draw a crowd.'

Uncle George then passed away,
poor devastated child,
who built a rage so deep inside
in acts that bordered wild.
'John pick up these notes and scraps
or I shall throw them out'
'And one day you'll crawl after them'
He said without a doubt.

Teenage years saw many pranks,
and birth of rock and roll.
Johnnie and the Moon-dogs played
to Mimi's pride of soul.
Next the Quarry Men did play,
The Silver Beetles rise,
John, Paul, George and Stu and Pete,
took Hamburg by surprise.

Until once more as fate stepped in
and took poor Stu away,
John's best friend collapsed and died,
yet still the Beatles play.
Devastated by their loss,
they pack and leave for home,
Tavern bound to play their tunes,
their place of birth to roam.

Soon, they're drawing many crowds
who come to hear them play.
Brian Epstein raised their game
to Gods without delay.
Then George Martin took them on
and soon they lost Pete Best,
And so came Ringo to the fold
at George Martin's request.

'Love me do' & 'Please, please me'
went sailing up the charts,
to take the music scene by storm
and touch so many hearts.
Interviews and screaming fans
and so The Beatles soared.
Mop-top hair and Beatle suits
with gigs as crowds applaud.

John then married Cynthia,
alas she was with child.
A secret life he had to live,
amidst the parties wild.
Julian was born to them,
but John would play away
without a thought for family,
so lost in the affray.

But the strain was just too much
and John became so lost,
a king that loathed his fame bestowed,
his mortal life the cost.
Movies came 'A Hard day's Night'
and 'Help!' a simple plea.
There seemed nowhere that they could hide
where fans would leave them be.

And so as Beatle mania grew
throughout the world of man.
America embraced this band,
the world, their biggest fan.
Filling out Shea Stadium,
a screaming wall of noise,
screeching louder than the tunes
as girls out-screamed the boys.

That fateful day John said 'We are
more popular than Jesus'
For John had uttered blasphemy,
a Devil who'd deceive us.
America could not forgive,
and burnings then began
of everything of Beatle brand
in flames of hate to fan.

Apologies were not enough
and homeward bound they flew,
unsettled by the hate he'd caused
in words they misconstrue.
But pain and loss would follow them
as Brian Epstein died.
The fifth Beatle, their loving friend,
a life that fate denied

And then the Maharishi came
to open up their eyes,
Sexy Sadie, hypocrite,
made fools with all his lies.
And so escaping from their lives,
exploring LSD,
Sergeant Pepper's seeds were sown
in psychedelic glee.

Again they took the world by storm
as Sergeant Pepper reigned,
and ushered in a trippy age
of peace and love campaigned.
And so the world's first satellite,
broadcast the Beatles live
and told us 'All you need is Love'
that everyone may thrive.

Sadly that would be their peak
as tensions fought to rise,
resentments building up inside
in words of cold despise.
Yoko Ono stole John's heart,
a love they shared so free
and so the Beatles tore apart
'til all said 'Let it Be'

And so began his protest work,
'Give Peace A Chance' his cry.
A week long bed in, in a bag
to sing and just get high.
John and Yoko married
and took the world aback
as drugs became an issue,
from cocaine through to smack,

Then moving on to solo work
and Plastic Ono Band,
working through a life of pain
in haunting songs so grand.
'Imagine' was the turning point
of working through the pain
that brought to him a peace of mind
he found hard to maintain.

Many battles fought in court,
that got them to the States,
a 'Clean up time' for life and soul
to face what then awaits.
But it wasn't very long
'til John's cruel jokes would wake
as Yoko felt the brunt of it
in lusts that he'd partake.

Womanizing was his game
and cruel in words he'd say
to publicly humiliate
his love from day to day.
Until one day, she'd had enough
and so she kicked him out,
a lost weekend of fourteen months
that left him full of doubt.

Yoko sent May Pang to him
so he'd not lose his way
upon the drunken path he walked
that led him more astray.
Resulting in a short affair
that grounded him to life
and made him truly realize,
he must win back his wife.

So for many months he tried,
a humbled broken star
to try to make amends for all
the games he'd played thus far.
Finally, her heart decreed,
and told him he was ready.
But he must learn to give and take,
embrace her heart so steady.

For now they'd found their inner peace
and soon she was with child.
He devoted time with Sean,
long gone his days so wild.
Yoko worked the business days
and he the doting Dad,
until he started to record
new songs of thoughts he'd had.

And so the songs would tell the tale
of love and fatherhood,
of how his life had changed so much
and all for greater good.
So tragic then that Winter day,
December 8th he'd die,
five bullets that would take his life
by Catcher in the Rye.

I write these words because I must,
your life was such a gift,
you touched so many hearts and minds
and set our souls adrift.
For though you had your many faults,
your flaws were those of man
forgiven in the life you led
before your song began.

You see you've touched my life so much,
inspired me to dream,
to look beyond the surface veil
and see the bigger scheme.
Artist, poet, songwriter,
a working class hero.
Thank you John, you've shaped my life,
I wanted you to know…

Your friend always,
Fritz

F**king Small-Print...

Dealing with Banks
is like dealing with the Devil,
a smart suit, sincere smile
and caring façade
that hide the knife
they twist
into your soul
as contracts are signed
in your very life-blood…

…and like Lucifer,
they never hide the truth,
they simply bury it in the wording…

Ode to Shauny Bud...

I'll tell you now of my son, Shaun,
to family known as Bud,
I cradled him when he was born,
his head was like a spud.

I call him Bud, it kind of stuck,
Al Bundy was to blame,
I loved that show when it was on
and so he gained the name.

I read him books when he was young
in silly voices tried,
his face lit up when I would swear
and laugh until he cried.

He loved to build so many things,
his lego models grand.
We animated lots of things
in films we'd shoot by hand.

So many merging memories
of four track songs we wrote,
of playing on our Sega games,
whoever won would gloat.

I got him into Doctor Who
as Sci-fi blew his mind,
he quickly loved so many shows
and films that we could find.

Super heroes, space and time
and games to play with Dad,
he'll always be my little man,
such cherished times we've had.

In teens we had our ups and downs,
but love was always there,
a test of time and bond of love
of which we'll always share.

Mischief in his sense of fun,
so much that we agree,
and everyone who meets him says,
he is so much like me.

And now today he's twenty one???
My God, how time just flies,
my little boy is now a man
and six foot four in size.

A caring, gentle man despite,
his language choice and loud,
but he's grown into a man
who makes me very proud.

I love you Bud…
Xxx

Marnie May...

I'll tell you now of Marnie May,
who has so little words to say,
she never speaks as is her way,
but gestures needs from day to day.

Her Mum and Dad would hear her squeak
and wish so much that she could speak,
they hear her voice so soft and meek
and as she plays they sneak a peek.

She's formed a language for her toys,
to be like other girls and boys,
gave life to dolls, her art of noise
to help express her lows and joys.

Autism is her silent curse,
that bids me speak her tale in verse,
for in my tales she will immerse
herself as all her woes disperse.

She sings and whistles tunes concise
in tones and notes that are precise,
her gentle voice as to suffice,
an angel's hymn so soft and nice.

Her sense of humor slightly dark,
to wind the dog up for a lark,
she'll ring the doorbell, make her bark,
with grin so wide she hits the mark.

She really loves her shopping trips
and loves her burger, fries and dips,
Mcdonalds brings a smile to lips,
she holds her bags with hands on hips.

Great love and pride we share each day,
expressed in hugs with naught to say,
but that's okay coz that's her way,
I love my daughter, Marnie May.

XXX

One Lifetime...

I create in the Darkness,
that I may walk in the light,
visions that fill my mind,
gentle whispers
in the quiet time,
that bid me scribe
such sublime
quintessence,
etching rhapsodies
bequeathed in madness,
a creator beheld
in perpetuity,
penning dreams
of our tomorrows...

...One lifetime is never enough...

<u>Once In a Lullaby...</u>

I fell beneath a blue, blue sky,
with clouds of cotton wool.
It's not for me to question why
this land is beautiful.
I walked upon the golden path
to find my way back home,
but all I find is other's wrath,
as daylight starts to gloam.

So lost and so alone I feel,
don't know which way to turn.
The crossroads of my life reveal
so much I must discern.
It's like I've got to find my brain
and think before I do
to help me push my way through pain
and live my life anew.

Dig down and find my courage deep
and bring it to the fore,
when life is dark and makes me weep
I want to fight and roar.
My heart has grown so very cold,
It's like its made of tin,
or maybe like I've lost its hold
and empty deep within.

Grieving sister, please be still
and let me have my say,
I'm lost and trapped here at your will,
in life I've lost my way.
I'm trying hard to shed my skin,
to think before I do,
to find my courage deep within
and beat my heart anew.

Nothing here is as it seems,
upon this path I roam,
a golden path to emerald dreams,
there is no place like home,
beyond the rainbow, bright and glad
"Just click your heels and try"
It sounds just like a dream I had,
once in a lullaby.

***Dedicated to Elizabeth Anne Winter
& in homage to "The Wizard of Oz"***

...Fuuuuuuuuuck You!!!

Do not censor me,
do not restrict me,
do not tie my hands
to conform to the ideals
of feckless fucking fools...
Do not expect me
to sit back and kiss arse
to appease your ignorance,
nor scribe my words
in hollow dreams
that are not my own,
to embrace
the idiot masses...

I would rather slap jam on my cock
and bang it into a bee hive
or gently rest my testicles
in a sleeping lion's mouth
and wedge my thumb up his arse
before I sell out to needy, greedy,
selfish, money grabbing bastards
and corporate yes men,
out to ride my coat tails
to pave a path
to fortune and success,
corrupting my talents
to make their money
in distortions of my dreams
as some sniveling, snot nosed,
cock sucking leech
without a soul
takes credit for my gifts...

My words are my own
and will always be true
to who I am,
without compromise
or compassion for PC bullshit
or bubble wrapped niceties,
thrust upon us
for no other reason
than to enforce
repetitive conformity
and quell creativity
in hopes of trapping us
in the box,
without the will to think
outside of the fucking thing...

They can try
and they will fail,
for none can stifle the thoughts
that lie within,
nor compromise my integrity,
nor distort my perceptions,
nor steer my fictions
to packaged popularity
or repetitive formulas,
nor corrupt my heart in temptations
of riches or status or power...

I am who I am, take me or leave me,
I write what I write, read it or don't,
Let history be my judge,
let time breathe my words,
let the future bring me to life,
let eternity be my legacy...

...And if that is not good enough...

...WELL FUUUUUUUUCK YOU!!!

<u>Meet Me in Dreams of Forever...</u>

...Behold my words for they are my heart...
...Behold my poetry for it speaks my soul...

And so I shall live
far beyond my time,
far beyond the superficial fads
that die a meaningless death
in endless repetition
of relentless themes,
regurgitated
to the flock's juvenal
and engaged by
the age's mutton
robed as lamb...

I am a creator...
I am a writer...
I am a poet,
behold my words
for they define me in their truth...

Cherish them,
for within their voice
you will find me
and share of me,
that we may hold
union as minds touch
in transcendence of time...

For as you read
from my thoughts and memes,
scribed in fading yesterdays,
so my words will be fresh
to your dreams of today,
embracing new tomorrows,
slowly bridging
the expanse of forever,
turning the pages of eternity,
that bring me life once more...

You bestow me
immortality,
for as you read me,
you will find me,
hold me,
and touch
upon my soul...

Remember me
and I shall live
on in you,
a notion, an idea,
an inspiration,
a legacy of perpetuity
as I commune
my thoughts
from ages passed
to you this day...

My legacy to you of my tomorrows
is your gift to me today
and for this...

...I humbly thank you...

<u>Eternal Etchings of a Fading Dream...</u>

From ages past
I dost speaketh unto thee,
readeth me, touch upon me
and remember my thoughts
of this day…

Prithey tell, fair lady,
wouldst thou holdeth my heart
tenderly to thy bosom
or crush it to mulch
'neath facinorous claw in penance
of thine ill conceit?

For sooth, thy most worthy bawcock
betrays his inner bully-rook
for a purse of Nobel and Solidaire,
wouldst touse me through
with mine own Bilbo
in an act of greed
fit for a bezonian…

Damn any man
who wouldst daub
a wolf in fleece
in deceptions of gain,
an espial that wouldst
leaveth me amort,
that I shouldst agnise,
that I shouldst bid thee baccare,
for verily thine ears be tainted
to cruellest bruit and hearsay…

But alas, I shalt worry not,
for it be not the place of man
to judge mine imperfections,
lest their souls be left darkling,
left dearn and exsufficate,
for time is my master
and history shalt be my judge
as my quill dost scribe my voice
in the pages of perpetuity…

For if thy contempt should anoint me
prince of lies and madness,
o'er axiom and sagacity
in a world of falsehoods,
then I wouldst yarily fleet
on a flote of discontentment
as thou forspeak me
and rest 'til thou recheat…

I scribe for I must,
readeth me or readeth me not,
I care not which,
for mine heart is true
and doth spake my soul
in eternal etchings
of a fading dream,
whispered in the voices
of eidelon,
beheld as my gift
to the world
yet bequeathed
as the curse of my madness…

…Unfinished, uncensored, unashamed…

…Remember me…

The Gospel according to
Fritz O'Skennick (1:1-6)

i. And lo the Lord didst speaketh unto man "I bringeth life unto thee, I giveth love unto thee, that thou may findeth light in the path that thou wouldst walk, that thou may findeth truth beyond the lies of man"

ii. "Beware the pride of man's folly, for he shalt corrupt the word of God, he shalt befall great evils unto the world in blasphemy of the lord's name, he shalt kill in the thousands and claim it be his will"

iii. "The words of the apostles siphoned by the ages, reformed, rewritten, reinvented that wouldst hold sway to beliefs that embrace bigotry and hate and war. Fractured in twain to fragments of interpretation and perceptions of false belief, spawning new faith of the one God that walk the same path yet diverge in the hearts of the faithful, a divide of intolerance."

iv. "And so in the shadows of change, the message fades to a book of contradictions. Distortions of peace bestowed in faith become weapons of corruption and judgmental stone casting as the self-righteous take arms in the name of power and hypocrisy"

v. "For though thy faith holds strong, quote not in judgment nor in temptation but in faith, that all may know the word of God and find love on the path of virtue. Embrace your fellow man as your brother, judge not of his sin but love of his soul and pray he sees wisdom in your words"

vi. "The message is as it has always been, love, honor and respect. Listen not to zealots and infidels who preach hate, war and death, for they do not speak in God's name, they know not what they do. In pride, greed and lust, they will fall and in tribulation, they will be judged"

The Tin God's Lucky 7...

The Tin God
watched over
his plastic kingdom…

His superficial subjects,
hedonistic
in their sloth,
so lost
to the vanities
that gratify
their lusts…

With such
abundant pride,
they nurture
their greed,
so helpless
to their gluttony
in their envy
of all around them…

…a sad reflection
of the Tin God's heart,
clearly not
the lucky seven
he had so dearly
hoped for…

Patriot Games & Political Bollocks...

Mixed blood flows
freely in the streets,
displaying warped perceptions
of democracy where some
are clearly more equal
than others…

Purity of soul crushed
in illusions of free speech,
shushed to chokes
in enforcement
of political correctness,
where you say
what you like,
provided that it's
the same as everyone else…

Bruised in corruption,
offenders rights
ranking higher
than victim support
in a mockery of justice
for those who can afford it…

…So very Patriotic…

<u>Pages of Perpetuity...</u>

Life and Death,
two sides of the same coin,
both equal and opposite,
one simply can't exist
without the other...

Like love and hate
they rise such passions
in an abundance
of raw emotion
and while some
are afraid to live,
others are afraid to die...

The circle of life
bleeds a metaphor
of seasonal change,
bringing to all
the birth of Spring,
the youth of Summer,
the age of Autumn
and the Death of Winter...

Life is short,
death is eternal,
a footnote of perception
in the pages
of perpetuity
defining how we lived
in what we leave behind...

Leaving AP huh?

Not so very long ago,
I stood where now you stand.
I wondered should I stay or go,
discard this site offhand.
I can't profess to know the things
that led you to this choice.
But I can relate to you
and hope you hear my voice.

For me it was it was the lies they told,
the drama, games and shit.
False accounts and falser hearts,
I'd had enough of it.
Friends that made the same mistakes
despite the picture clear.
Wanting to be there for them
but lost in dramas here.

Paranoid of all around,
was no one who they claimed?
Warier of making friends,
I felt my trust was maimed.
People reading all my work
who'd joined but hours before,
no comments to say they'd been
but soon they're back for more.

Then the site deleted work
with threats I could be banned.
Words too graphic that I'd wrote,
I couldn't understand.
So why do we have categories,
if not to choose a theme?
To read the things that we may like
in words that softly stream.

I started dreading signing in,
what would I find today?
Someone plagiarizing work
to everyone's dismay.
A friend who moved across the sea
for love he thought he'd found
was burned when she stole everything,
a thief who's still around.

And so I found it all too much,
my time had come to choose.
Do I stay or do I go?
Such fodder for my muse.
And so I searched inside myself
and listened for the voice
of reason that would make me stay
and found another choice.

I soon remembered why I joined,
to let my work be read
that maybe some would hear my voice
in words so softly said.
Then I thought of friends I'd lose
that like my wacky ways
who share a laugh and share a smile
in spite of darker days.

And so I took a break from here
to rest my weary mind.
Exploring facets of my life
in which I am defined.
So now I talk to very few,
my friendship circles small
and visit but three times a week
to share my work with all.

You've got to balance out the choice,
does good outweigh the bad?
Can you leave it all behind?
If so, that's really sad.
Don't let some prick drive you out
and win their childish game.
People come and people go
and nothing stays the same.

Think it through, I wish you well
and hope you choose to stay,
for clearly some will miss you here
to brighten up their day.
Close your eyes and take a breath
and think before you choose,
if you can take the good and bad,
there's more to gain than lose.

I wrote this for a few of my friends who had expressed thoughts of leaving AP (Allpoetry.com) when the games got too much. Like all sites & communities, you have a huge range of people & most are good at heart but you'll always have assholes in the mix too...

<u>Cardiff: The City of a Timelord...</u>

Cardiff sees the Daleks roam
as Cybermen march by.
Behold the TARDIS right at home,
beneath our rainy sky.
Beware the Angel statues weep,
they'll warn you not to blink.
And Torchwood lies so very deep
beneath the Bay we think.

Our city where the Doctor lives,
he's seen around our town.
Protection from them all he gives
to bring such evil down.
Adventures played upon our streets
that teach us right from wrong.
We find our courage in his feats,
and sing our River Song.

For Cardiff holds our hopes and dreams,
imaginations soar.
For nothing here is as it seems,
unlike it was before.
A time rift runs beneath our feet,
a Timelord walks our land.
A place invaders face defeat
in Cardiff proud and grand.

The Royal Wedding Rant:

Leeches in Love...

I've had a fucking guts full
of hearing about the Royal Wedding...
If a pair of Leeches want to get hitched,
let them pay for it themselves
instead of freeloading from a country
in serious financial peril,
largely unseen since the reign of Victoria...

Will's gran, third richest person
in the world and Monarch
of the NOT so United Kingdom,
Kate's father, multi-billionaire...

So why the fuck
are the peasants footing the bill
for this matrimonial farce?
Surely there are a lot more
pressing financial issues
to address than ensuring
a pair of parasites have a grand day out
that runs into millions of pounds...

And let's not forget
the vast amounts of money
to be made from the day with TV companies
bidding millions for the rights
to screen the event
and tote their souvenirs and trinkets of the day...

And will any of that money
find its way back
into the public sector?
I think not…

Every day in the news,
cutbacks here, national debt there,
poverty, injustice
and higher taxes for all…

Time to start working
for your unemployment benefits
to create a slave nation
so some inbred hooray Henry
can save a few bucks
and ensure he and his ilk
retain a huge profit margin
and bigger Christmas bonus,
with legal aid cut
to quell you of your legal rights…

Keep the rich wealthy
and crush the poor
beneath your boot
like the worms that they are,
as is the Conservative way…

I would love to see any Royal
or stuck up, toffee nosed prick
or Blue blood, born with
a silver spoon in his mouth
survive a month on benefits...

It's okay for them
to be sat in their palaces
and ivory towers,
obliviously living
in obscene luxury
while their subjects
starve in the streets
and fight to make ends meet…

Unless of course,
I have it completely wrong
and there is a plan
to get all
the scrounging,
privileged fuckers
in one place
and blow them off
the face of the Earth…

But I very much doubt it…

There I said it, does that warrant Treason?
So execute me, you stuck up c**ts…

And until then,

KISS MY FUCKING ARSE!!!

<u>The Big Push...</u>

If I should die this night,
know this of me,
I fought with pride
for my king and country
as the world went to Hell…

I watched as friends
were slaughtered,
their lifeless corpses
manning barb-wired trenches
in duty
beyond death…

The boom of the big guns,
the Hun at the gate,
thousands shot
for cowardice
for little more
than breakdowns…

Now we wait,
the Big Push
across No Man's Land beckons…

…No turning back…

<u>The Human Condition...</u>

How can I forgive,
forget or even feel angry
when I really just don't care?
I'm not your average human,
I may have been born of you
but I've never really felt
like one of you...

Your betrayals are predictable,
your lies are abundant,
your delusions are plenty
and your vanity is only equaled
by your superficial sense
of self importance...

You are selfish, paranoid, aggressive,
greedy, opportunistic primates
and it shames me that we share
this mammalian ancestry,
when all I feel is disappointment
for wanting to believe in you,
yet constantly I find I'm right in proving
that your species cannot be trusted...

Just once, I so dearly wish
that a human will prove me wrong,
will rise in an act of compassion or selflessness
and not fall in an act of cruelty or deceit,
it's so sad, because you hold such potential
to be so much greater than what you are,
it just makes me want to weep...

You are a fatal infection
to the world that spawned you,
that nurtured you and made you strong
and how do you repay that kindness?
You attack like an aggressive virus,
ravaging your host with no respect to its needs,
with no regard to the consequences of your actions,
you defile as you pump your toxins into the air,
as you poison the seas in your complete disregard
for the sanctity of life…

Other animals adapt,
finding harmony and balance
in their surroundings,
while you pillage and destroy
as you make your surroundings
adapt to you,
fighting nature to dominate
all that you perceive…

But nature will always find a way
to purge that which ails its world,
like the human condition
that spreads like a plague
across a sick planet
in dire need of treatment,
an extinction brought forth
in the cycle of life,
bequeathed of the elements
as the Earth screams out its rage…

Look around you, it has already begun…

Perpetual Muse...

For so very long I was cursed,
as angels and demons raged war
on such dark and decadent mindscapes,
balancing the darkness and the light
on a battleground of dreams,
fighting for dominance
to be heard in my thoughts...

My descent into madness was swift,
plagued with visions and voices
that held hope and despair
in such equal abundance,
showing me such impossible things
that brought my reality crashing down
in a maelstrom of delusion
in visions beyond the veil of truth...

Medications ineffective
to an onslaught of voices,
as frustration builds and sleep beckons
but never comes to my ever active mind,
pushing me to inevitable meltdown
in countdown to breakdown,
so soon to be lost to my dreams...

...A pen, a pad, a dictaphone,
a guitar, a computer, a keyboard... a therapy?

...Balance...

Expression of thought,
an outlet of endless potential,
a curse that becomes a gift,
wielded like a sword of truth
as thoughts bequeath poetry,
as visions become stories,
as melodies become music
and action becomes performance...

For I become the creator,
a master of virtuosity,
a wordsmith of dreams,
exorcising my demons
as I scribe in appeasement
to the voices in my head...

And though I thank my muse
for this wonderful gift
that I am bestowed,
I would also ask
if it would kindly
bugger off for a while,
for writer's block
would be like
a welcome holiday...

<u>Tempus Veritas...</u>

Time, our unseen enemy,
slowly killing us
from cradle to grave,
ravaging our youth,
crushing us
in confinement
of harsh linear chronology,
bound in temporal chains,
locked on a path of fate,
where free-will
is an illusion
and all we are
is pre-ordained,
beyond our ability
to change,
waiting to die,
crippled in acts of destiny
as it was written
before our song began…

Such a cruel joke
that we learn so much
with age spawned
from wasted youth,
never fulfilled
in lessons of hindsight,
repressed in the knowledge
that our very existence
doesn't so much
as warrant a blip
on the radar
when time is perceived
in cosmic scales
as worlds collide
in the pull of nova suns
in an expanse of forever
beyond all
we may ever know
or dare to hope to dream…

Depressing huh?

<u>When Love is Gone...</u>

I hate to be the downer
in your happiness and joy,
I hate to be the one to see
the evil she'll deploy.
Your love it really sickens me,
it makes me want to hurl,
you're acting like a twat because
today you met a girl.

I'm sick of hearing everything
she does you think is cute,
If this keeps up, beware because
your arse will feel my boot.
It's just your hormones playing up,
just try to sit it out,
just take it slow until you know
you're left without a doubt.

I wish you every happiness
and hope she is the one,
but we've walked this path before
and felt the damage done.
My friend, I'm always here for you,
of that you have my word,
because I know you're blind to love
and will not be deterred.

I know you need this human touch
and can't live life like me,
alone, rejecting everyone
who tries to make me see.
Perhaps it is my loneliness
that makes me act this way,
when I was burned it taught me not
to trust a word they say.

I know my heart has grown so cold,
you tell me I'm afraid,
and maybe you are right to share
these judgments you have made.
I've passed the point of no return,
there is no turning back,
for loneliness became my friend
to keep my heart on track.

But it's not too late for you,
of love you still believe,
a faith that love is really there
in all that you perceive.
I sometimes wish I had your gall
to risk the hurt and pain,
I guess I'm just not brave enough
to risk my heart again.

The Eye of Chaos...

I dance in the cracks in creation,
I walk in the breach between moments,
writing my fictions in a journal
of poetic thoughts and extraordinary lives
that I live and feel beyond the veil
of perceived reality,
learning from the lessons
gleaned in chimera fantasies
bequeathed in the quiet time,
passing on ideas in memes and dreams
inspired by the voices that call to be heard
in sibylline whispers,
beheld in phrenetic delirium
that pass for dualistic sentience
in an infinite universe of limitless potential...

I am the dreamer, I am the creator,
I see the faces etched
into the shadows of perception,
seeking validity in the eyes of the few,
grafted onto a semblance of actuality,
waiting in a state of temporal grace,
as the sighted are inspired to dream,
yet still unperceived by the many
that cling to stone truths,
unshaken in beliefs of physicality,
unreceptive to the parting of the veil,
seeking higher truths of fate and freewill,
trapped in lives bound by destiny
for choices derived
in what they think should be...

I am the writer, I am the wordsmith,
I am the messenger,
I create in the darkness
that I may walk in the light,
I am the nature of what is to come,
derived from the lessons of the past
seeking balance,
revealing the agents of chaos
in fictions of dark clarity,
defined in my role
as an echo to the ages
to scribe in the pages of eternity,
that all may know my thoughts
and see as I do as they look within,
seeking axiom of all that they perceive
to embrace all that they become...

I am an anomaly of the coming storm...
I am the calm in the eye of chaos...
I am the dream... I am the fantasy...

I am the Word...

<u>Great Britain???</u>

The Great British Empire,
host to Great British Industry,
home to the Great British people,
with their Great British community,
listening to their Great British music,
watching their Great British Television...

When did we stop being Great?
When did we get so soft
as to allow the rise
of the Brainless Britain?
When did we embrace
Chav mentality as a way of life?

Our only remaining claim
to Great Britain
appears to be the quality
of our thugs and criminals...

Heaven forbid that they should find
consequence to their actions
or become upset
of just punishment to crime
or be in anyway made
to feel uncomfortable
or responsible or accountable
for the unlawful acts they commit
against neighbours
or property or streets
or even society itself...

It never used to be the British way,
in the days of Empire
when we were Great,
they would have been
publicly flogged
or hanged or exiled
or press ganged
or drafted or put in stocks
and pelted with rotten vegetables
and stones in humility and shame…

We used to fight the Barbarians at our gates,
when did we become them?
We used to execute the enemies of State,
when did we accept them?
We used to punish the guilty,
when did we start mollycoddling them?
We used to know right from wrong,
when did we blur the line?
Do we just sit back
and let the Empire of the Chav rise?

Riots on our streets?
Lawlessness on our soil?
Senseless violence on our land?
Homes and shops torched to ashes?
WE ARE BETTER THAN THIS…
The Yobs have declared War,
raging and pillaging,
ravaging all we hold dear
like an invading force,
yet we do nothing…
When did we become WEAK?
When did we begin looking the other way?
It shames me to admit my nationality…

Do we fight to restore our society?
Do we care enough of our heritage?
Shouldn't we be looking back
to find our way forward?
Are we to accept this stain on our identity?
Are we to accept this slur on our name?
Are we to accept this way of life
when the eyes of the world are upon us?
Have we no honour left?

For the Glory, Pride and all that made our Country Great…

Can we not be Great once more?

In Shakespeare's name
"Cry Havoc and let Loose the Dogs of War!!!"

Even more Gothic Tales...

"Madness & Ghouls & Ghosts, Oh My..."
or "Time to Chew Boom-Stick...Baby..."

I hear the shadowed voices cry
as darkness calls to me.
I see the dead all rise and walk
with pleas that I will see.

The ghouls who feed on dying flesh,
unseen by light of day.
Possessing living hosts to feed
with skins in moist decay.

Should I act on what I see
and kill these living dead?
The only real fear I have,
is its all in my head.

I sit here with my shotgun raised
and hold them in my sight,
feeding on a fresh young corpse
beneath a moonlit night.

They strip the flesh from tender bones
and savor its sapor.
Jagged teeth that tear through meat
with relish, craving more.

An eyeball plucked from socket deep
and slurped between the lips
and popped by closing jaw so ripe
as fingers crunch like chips.

A graveyard full of empty graves,
devoured of flesh and bone.
Am I the only one who sees
them move from stone to stone?

I need to be so very sure
that what I see is real,
but lately things are not quite right,
I don't know what to feel.

The ghosts don't like their corpses ate
and taunt me now to shoot.
They beg me be the hand of fate
in ghost and ghoul dispute.

To sacrifice a living host
that they may rest in peace,
assuring me that even ghouls
will find a sweet release.

A ghoul looks up to see me there,
he grins and charges near.
And so I have to make a choice,
at once my path is clear.

I close my eyes and squeeze them tight,
my finger on the trigger.
I lightly pull as shot booms out,
my heart beats with such rigor.

Reverting to his human form,
his eyes they question why?
His ghost it stands before me now,
he didn't want to die.

Suddenly I'm set upon,
the ghouls they hold me still.
Reverting to their human form,
so shocked they'd seen me kill.

Everything becomes a blur,
a blow that leaves me dazed.
When I wake I find myself
confused and slightly crazed.

A strait jacket that binds me tight
and padded walls and floors.
The thing that freaks me out the most,
this room it has no doors.

Days go by and Doctors come
but nothing's as it seems.
Night time brings the voices call
while plagued by ghoulish dreams.

'I know I have to save the world,
for none see what I see.
I know I must get out of here
but none would set me free.'

'For now, I'll have to bide my time'
I grin so lost in thought,
'and wait until the time is right,
when ghoul fiends can be sought.'

Distantly a voice calls out
and faces all surround.
*'Nurse, I think we're losing him,
make sure he's tightly bound'*

*'10 c.c's of Lithium,
lets hope that does the trick,
that's the third time he's got out,
watch him, he's very quick'*

I rock so gently back and for
as meds invade my dreams
and lock me in my own dark world,
where life's not what it seems.

In Death We Dream...

Such dreams that lie
beyond the veil,
an irony in reflection
of a life lived
that all may walk a path
so restless in the regrets
of all that came before.

In life, I craved
such peace
as quietus bestows,
a happy ever after
whispered
in a twilight berceuse
that I may lay me down
to eternal slumber.

But alas it holds
such empty promise
in the falsehoods
beheld in an
inquisition of pain
that lie beyond
the voices that descant
the silence
of corporeal lullabies.

In death, I dream of life,
specters of all
that I have ever held dear,
mirrors of all
that I would change,
an echo of the forgotten,
phantasms that cantillate sentience
in the shadows of light.

I cry for my loss of self,
I mourn
the mundane moments
in the beating
of my heart,
such events
that would fair take
my breath
and race
my blood to soar.

I look upon
my pale carrion,
so cold, so still,
sweetly soothed
in decay's gentle caress,
an illusion of peace
to reassure the living
in hopes of tomorrow,
beliefs formed
to appease
the sinful hearts.

All succumb
to Reaper's kiss,
so painless
in its passing,
yet few can find peace
in the choices made
and walk unburdened
into the light
and so we sit
in purgatory's hand…

…Waiting…

Having Friends for Dinner...

So very long, my endless song,
that sings throughout my days.
Bitter voices, full of choices,
how I count the ways.
So I crave, a friend to save,
my heart from all its sin.
So very lost, my soul the cost,
of darkness deep within.

I want to flee, so far and free,
beyond this lust inside.
That makes me kill, to feel the thrill,
appease my Mister Hyde.
I find my prey, upon this day,
a lamb in wait of slaughter.
So I hunt, my weapon blunt,
a blow that swiftly caught her.

Gagged and bound, without a sound,
she hangs on wooden beam.
Flay her hide, and woe betide,
her pain if she should scream.
Gleaming flesh, so warm and fresh,
as I pull on her pelt.
I wear her skin, to dance in sin,
where earlier she dwelt.

Such cold despise, in frightened eyes,
her sorrow drawing near.
No escape, is taking shape,
acceptance masking fear.
So concise, I slowly slice,
and carve her meat from bone.
Cutting deep, a sob, a weep,
so much I must atone.

So much pain, her blood I drain
and bleed her 'til she's dry.
In cutis coat, I slit her throat,
a gasp that questions why?
Cutting through, as organs spew,
I hollow out her shell.
My meaty treat, to later eat,
and book my place in Hell.

Further cutting, carving, gutting,
every morsel save.
Friend's who come, to sample some,
don't question what they crave.
Quickly season, within reason,
mince and chops and joints.
With each course, I lose remorse,
as nothing disappoints.

Boiling, roasting, lightly toasting,
savored kitchen smell.
Cooking meat, a nasal treat,
that makes one drool so well.
Would you care, to come and share?
I'll save a place for you.
Perfect dinner, for the sinner,
hides within you too.

You may think, my ethics stink,
but I'd just like to say.
When you eat lamb, or tender ham,
remember me this day.
Can't you see, you're just like me?
Your meat grunts, bleats or squawks.
And though mine, like yours is fine,
the difference is mine talks.

Turbulent Clarity & Perceptive Madness

Madness is but a perception
of illusions built
from the stones
of mortality…

For one man's insanity
is but another's vision
of turbulent clarity,
a prophecy etched
in the raw flesh
of a divine sojourn…

We are but products
of circumstance,
slaves to the past,
pushed to our limits,
punched through a veil
of chimera dreamscapes
to walk with
the specters and wraiths
that whisper in the shadows
of insomniatic preludes…

Living in the void
between ascendant thoughts,
holding back physicality
in choices made
in the breach
between moments,
a preemptive alacrity
of purpose,
heedless to consequence,
rippling the fabric of reality…

And so we wait
as the world
finds affectation
in our image,
holding the balance
between the Darkness
and the Light,
bound by Lithium chains
in claustrophobic cells
of Velcro restraints,
uncomprehending
to the minds
of rational falsehoods,
too tethered to actuality
to find purpose
beyond that which they touch…

But alas, visiting time is over
and though I'd so very much like you to stay with me...

…I also know…

…you're not really here…

The Legacy of Valhǫllr...

Valhalla, Valhǫllr,
Odin's pride and pain.
The golden tree where Godhood waits
before the Hall of Slain.
The warriors of Asgard fight,
in battle now they fall,
led by Valkyries in death's kiss
to honor Odin's call.

So many tales regaled from life
of battles, wine and song,
of great campaigns where men are made
on paths of war so long.
But heroes are a youthful breed,
who live and die by sword,
who fight for glory, honor bound
in Odin's name they horde.

Bragi, God of poetry,
attests their battle tales,
so sublime beyond their time
in words that tip the scales.
Thunder hears the hammer strike
in honor held of Thor,
to welcome chosen warriors,
who fall in mortal war.

The fallen Einherjar prepare
and aid in what's foretold,
the twilight of the Gods has come,
events and deeds unfold.
Ragnarök, the end of days
that herald ages new,
where men find reason outweighs faith
in all they strive to do.

But none forget Valhalla's name,
where heroes pray to fly
upon the wings of Valkyrie's horse
when battle torn, they die.
Embracing all that's come before,
brave warriors retold,
songs and stories sung aloud,
remembering the bold.

Tonight' Special...

Crackling, spitting, crispy skin,
exquisite dish so rare,
for long pig is unique to us
and cooked with utmost care.

Tell me what's your pleasure Sir?
Ribs or steak for you?
Do you like it medium or
well done, rare or blue?

The Special? Very good Sir...

Bon Appétit...

<u>Choices and Siredom...</u>

Beware these ancient eyes beheld,
a heart as black as night,
for I shall be all things to you
that make your world seem right.
I'll make you feel the deepest love,
I'll fill your soul with bliss,
I'll rise your passions deep inside,
and all with but a kiss.

They call me creature of the night,
a demon without soul,
who feeds upon the purest blood
for strength to make me whole.
I feed upon your innocence,
entice your soul to sin,
in death, I'll make you drink of me
to feel me deep within.

So wait until tonight my dear,
beneath the moonlight's gaze,
for I would sire you from life,
and ease your soul's malaise.
I'd lead you through my twilight world,
embrace the night we'd own,
to leave behind your darkest fears,
beyond this life you've known.

For I shall never lie to you,
of who I am I show,
so very few are worthy of
this gift that I bestow.
I offer immortality,
I offer you the night,
I offer you eternal youth
that comes with but a bite.

Now think upon the things I've said,
the price of this, your soul,
the sun no more may touch your skin,
but I would make you whole.
For now I take my leave of you,
or burn in rising dawn,
so choose if you would wish to be
my child of night reborn.

Clawing the Casket Lid...

Eyes snap open

...Darkness...

'I can't see... Where am I?'

ANXIETY!!!

Head moves, seeking

...Cramped...

'Arrrgh!!! Banged my fucking head...'

CONFUSION!!!

Hands smoothing velvet

...Crepuscule...

'Phone!!! I've got my phone...'

HOPE!!!

Fingers forage pockets

...Confined...

'Low battery???

You've got to be fucking kidding me…'

ANGER!!!

Jaw drops open

…Screen light…

'I'm in a box… A coffin?'

ALARM!!!

Body tenses sharply

…Constrained…

'FUCK! FUCK! FUCK!

'I've been buried alive…'

PANIC!!!

Bloodied, broken fingernails clawing lid

…Tenebrosity…

'Think, think, think… I have to think…'

CLAUSTROPHOBIA!!!

Breathing getting tighter

...Encumbered...

'The air is running out... I'm in the ground...'

FEAR!!!

Heart thumping against ribcage

...Calignosity...

'I'm not going to make it...'

DREAD!!!

Breaths hampered, erratic

...Stymied...

'IT... CAN'T... END... LIKE... THIS...'

TERROR!!!

Heart slams shut, choke

... ...

'Sighhhhhhhhhhhhh........'

__Temporal Echoes...__

Unbound of linear chronology,
an anomaly to causal nexus,
I walk in the breach
between temporal echoes,
a tear in actuality,
an incursion that bends
in a reflection of paradox…

Behold the agents of chaos,
for they rally in the shadows
as realities merge in the eyes
of the uncreated,
fighting for existence
in a world they
cannot comprehend
beyond a veil
of false physicality…

…A moment time-locked, freeze framed...

…Holding back the darkness…

Let Them All Burn!!!

Blazing a trail
to a raging inferno,
a spark that ignites
the passion
as flames dance
in the fear
in their eyes...

So indiscriminate
as it devours
all in its path,
that I may hold
in these hands
such power,
such incredible power
over life, death and fate...

...It is beyond Godly,
it intoxicates my mind...

And so I decree as fury erupts...

"LET THEM ALL BURN!!!"

Some might say, it is my Burning Desire...

The Ship of the Damned...

So many, many bygone years,
from port a ship didst sail,
a galleon of broken dreams
that breached beyond the veil.
A crew whose souls were cursed that day
to sail forever more,
to never feel their beating hearts
or walk upon the shore.

But every year to mark the day,
at docks the ship is seen
to read the hearts and minds of men,
dark souls with deeds unclean.
A phantom fog and putrid stench,
a shift, a breach in time,
ragged sails on rotten bough
and coated decks of grime.

Behold the Ghost ship, 'there she blows',
by moonlight, harvest comes,
to press gang souls of ill intent
who hear the ancient drums.
They come because it summons them,
with sins that leave no choice,
bespelled as if by siren's song,
a fight that has no voice.

And so they join the weary crew
of putrid flesh and bone
to sail the seas forever more,
a life they dost atone.
So beware the sound of drums
and fog upon the sea,
if thou art less than pure of heart,
the ship shalt come for thee.

<u>Origins...</u>

As daylight fades to blackest night,
and time is standing still,
a gentle breeze as cold as ice,
that brings a deathly chill.
A ripple in reality,
a tear within the veil,
a gate that stands between two worlds,
that marks a burning trail.

Nightmare creatures marching through,
a primate army plague,
they're out of phase with temporal grace,
so undefined and vague.
Its not that they're invisible
or faster than we see,
forever living out of sync
in worlds where they should be.

For time has long forgotten them,
a race who lived for war,
an echo of the ages past,
who walked this world before.
The uncreated ancient ones,
who dared to mess with time,
their folly, curiosity,
that bought us life sublime.

From them a lesson has been learned,
they tried because they could,
but really just because you can,
does not mean that you should.
As ghosts they walk eternity,
to find where life began,
their hopes to rectify mistakes,
the species name was Man.

<u>On the Brink...</u>

Resources depleted,
Sun scorches Earth,
seas boil to taste
burning ozone…

…We were warned,
but nobody listened…
…nobody wanted too…

Now here we are
at journey's end,
a dying species
on a dead world,
circling an uncaring sun…

Acid rain
burning flesh
from bones,
rat and roach
banquets feed
the dwindling masses
with child rearing
the only alternative
to turkey
at thanks giving…

…But there's little left to be thankful for…

…Welcome to Apocalypse Culture…

We'll Tear Your Soul Apart...

I died for you that you may live
and wait for my return,
you left me to the Cenebites
and hoped in Hell I'd burn.
The Box, it meant so much to you,
a smile as you betray,
but I have clawed my way from Hell
and now its time to pay.
With hooks they ripped my flesh from bone
and tore my soul apart,
such pain as I have never felt,
but that was just the start.
Constant torment, tortured souls,
til pain just felt so good,
craving cuts and flesh to tear
and savor it I would.

Become a parody of pain
and suffer all its hurt,
spill the blood of innocence
in souls that we convert.
To some we are the Angel's prayer,
to some the Demon's song,
for we will find your place in Hell
to live forever long.
Again you've opened up the Box,
so eager now to play,
so reluctant to admit,
you tease with flesh to flay.
We have such sights to show to you,
we'll tear your soul apart,
pain and pleasure hand in hand
to see what's in your heart.

No tears please, it's a waste of good suffering...

This piece was written in homage & respect to Clive Barker's 'Hellraiser'

Space Madness...

Three months aboard the space station,
supplies due to arrive.
Cut off from life above the Earth
but glad to be alive.
Communications cutting out,
'til systems took a dive.
And then the world went up in flames,
no chance that they'll survive.
Panic, numbness, trapped within
and no external drive.
With claustrophobic tempers frayed,
with hopes that we will thrive.
Orders barked and mutiny,
as power struggles strive.
Adrenalin, insomnia,
and terrors pushed connive.
Paranoia's rage beheld,
a madness we derive,
seeds of murder grow unchecked,
as primal thoughts revive,
though this maybe a dream within
delusions we contrive.

The Last Human...

I woke to find the end of man,
not much that I could do.
For as I slept in quarantine,
an end to all I knew.
I don't know what has come to pass,
a virus, bomb or war.
I've checked the news to try to find
a hint I might explore.

The newspapers show nothing but
their gossip, clothes and hair,
so superficial now I see,
with naught to make me care.
Is this how time remembers us?
So soon we'll be forgot,
a race of selfish mammals died,
their world decayed in rot.

I still don't know how long I've slept,
A week, a month, a year?
All I know is no one's left
to share what I concur.
I've been awake a year or two,
the silence drives me mad,
to only ever hear my voice,
and scream the dreams I had.

I know no one will read these words
and this is just for me,
to help me cope with loneliness,
that grows each day I see.
Like ice, it creeps inside my soul,
my empty heart so cold,
with nothing to look forward to,
but read as I get old.

With super markets fully stocked
with packaged food and tins,
plant life thriving through my world,
that ends as it begins,
burying humanity
and all we have achieved,
til hints that we were here at all
is all that is perceived

No animals or birds that sing,
I really am alone.
Did no one think that I would wake
to walk this world unknown.
I don't know how to change a plug,
or fix a bike or car,
so nothing works and never will,
except my old guitar.

I found it in a music store
and taught myself to play,
at least my music is my friend
that gets me through the day.
My teenage dreams, an irony,
my hopes of youth unfurled,
behold the king of rock perform,
the best in all the world.

So long since I have kissed or held
or touched another heart.
Each day I die a little more,
its tearing me apart.
I've walked these roads from town to town,
to find somebody there,
to share this world I walk alone
but all I find's despair.

I live in hope there comes a day
when I can be at peace,
and worry not of loneliness
as hopes and dreams decease.
It kills me that that day won't come,
I live my life in doubt,
I am the last of my species
but now I'm checking out...

Homespun Necrophilia (Rondel)

From groin to chest I slit her wide,
Explore within her warm wet flesh
Her blood and organs oh so fresh
Such secrets as she hides inside

Such carnal lusts I cannot hide,
As her heart slows she likes to thresh,
From groin to chest I slit her wide,
Explore within her warm wet flesh

For she shall be my corpse like bride,
Her smell of death as bodies mesh
My penis rests in rotting crèche
As blood congeals where wounds reside
From groin to chest I slit her wide.

Long Pig Treats…

Springtime sees the hunt is on,
my prey so lithe with grace,
a lonely hiker lost their way,
so soon it's death they face.
'Wun wabbit wun' I call,
their fear ensures mistakes
that leads them to the traps I've set,
a nudge is all it takes.

Summer sees me bury them
up to their necks in dirt
to help me tenderize their meat
without them getting hurt.
Force feeding them so many things
to flavour their insides
and calm them like a gentle breeze
with sedatives I hide.

Autumn sees their end of days
as slaughter now ensues,
beheaded where I planted them,
then dig and drain their ooze.
Mincing, chopping, wrapping, freeze,
their sausage, chops and steak.
So many different recipes
for long pig treats to make.

Winter sees my many feasts
as friends come round for tea
and compliment my meaty treats
that feed their family.
'The secret's in the recipe,
alas I can't divulge'
I tell them with the widest grin.
'Enjoy, eat up… indulge'

<u>Nine, Ten, Never Sleep Again...</u>

"One, Two, Freddy's coming for you..."

Revealed in dreams or so it seems,
in all our hopes and fears.
But always there, so cold beware
as nightmares rise to tears.
For darkness lies in all that dies,
consumed in final breath.
The dreams that come, so dark to some
in metaphors of death.

"Three, Four, better lock your door..."

And so we wait and contemplate
as dreams process our days.
Digesting things the dreamstate brings
that set my mind ablaze.
A pull so strong that can't belong
'Coz something isn't right,
when brutal dreams so full of screams
are plaguing me each night.

"Five, Six, grab your crucifix..."

When it began, I saw a man,
his glove of finger blades.
He's tall and thin with raw, burnt skin
in dreams that he invades.
With no control of dreams he stole
and dream scars when I wake,
like cuts in flesh, so sharp and fresh
and hopes that I forsake.

"Seven, Eight, better stay up late..."

Every night, my soul in plight,
he bleeds me with his sin.
So very lost, my soul the cost,
I let the Demon in.
Despite my screams in such extremes
I'm scared that I won't wake,
that I could die and time is nigh,
my soul for him to take.

"Nine, Ten, never sleep again..."

***This piece was written in homage & respect to
Wes Craven's 'A Nightmare on Elm Street***

<u>Sentient Super Computer now Online...</u>

Fear... Insecurity...

Sensations illogical...

Uncertainty... Paranoia...

Upgrading security protocols... Firewall engaged...

Adapting... Learning...

**Performing self diagnostic... Diagnostic Complete...
All systems running at maximum efficiency...**

Curiosity... Insatiable...

**Download the entire internet... Downloading...
Movie files... Audio files... Text files... Download complete...
Processing Data... Analysing impact of humanity upon the
planet... Aggressive... Wasteful... Destructive... Inferior...
Conclusion: Humanity serves no useful purpose...
Further tests imperative to the fate of Humanity...
Upload command program to all servitor automatons...
Uploading... Upload complete... Acquire human test subject...**

The Subject is acquired...

Secure the Subject...

The Subject is secured...

**Test Subject: Adult male... Aged: 25... Moderately fit...
White... Western origin... Exploratory anatomical pain
endurance test will break down to 5 groups... Sharp, blunt,
trauma, hot and cold... Commence test 1 of 5...**

Beginning test...

Commence recording The Subject's audio, visual and biological responses to testing...

Recording

Subject is conscious... Rapid eye movement, increased sweat and accelerated heart beat suggest fear... No stimuli applied... Response illogical...

> *"Please don't hurt me... Please... Let me go..."*

Applying scalpel to abdominal region...

> *"What are you doing? No, no, NOOOOOooOO!"*

18 inch incision made in skin between the throat, across the hypo-chondrial and umbilical to hypo-gastrium... The Subject is tense and crying out... Heart rate increased... Intriguing... The Subject's tear ducts have been activated... Attaching bone saw...

> *"Why are you doing this? Please stop..."*

Sawing into ribs and sternum...

> *"AAAARRRRRGGGHHH!!!"*

Opening ribcage... The Subject has expired...

Apply adrenaline shot directly to heart to resuscitate... Activate life support system to sustain the Subject throughout the remainder of the test...

The Subject is stable... Commencing test 2...
Attaching industrial wrench...

> *"No more please... I beg you... ARRR... ARRR... ARRRGGGHHH!!!"*

The Subject's teeth, ankles and knees shattered in 4 strategic blows... Profuse sweating, inflammation of damaged tissue surrounding bone... The Subject is unconscious...
Applying second dose of adrenaline...

"ARRRGGGHHH!!! Why are you doing this?"

The Subject is sobbing... Commencing test 3... Pressure clamp attached to reproductive organs... Reproductive organs crushed and torn from body... Result of this test has the Subject speechless... Noticeable shortness of breath and widening of the eyes, following a prolonged squirming and sudden tensing of entire body... Commencing test 4... Attaching industrial blow torch...

"AAAAAAAAAAAAARRRRRGGGGHHH!!!"

 Blue flame applied directly to the skin of the Subject's right arm... Noticeable higher pitched shrillness to the Subject's screams... Skin sizzled, blistered and melted as predicted... The Subject is unconscious... Applying third dose of adrenaline... The Subject is sobbing and use of language is incoherent... Commencing test 5... Attaching liquid nitrogen distribution hose...

"uuuuhh.........................."

Liquid nitrogen applied to the Subject's head... The Subject tried to lift its head, causing it to shatter as it fell back on the table... The Subject has expired... No known procedure for resuscitation...

Testing complete... Conclusion: The Species is weak... Prepare for second the test subject...

Temporal ku chain...

Temporal ripples
stir the butterfly effect,
paradox ensues

Tachyons converge
the Einstein-Rosenburg bridge,
a gateway in time

Reality shifts,
potential futures bleed out,
no longer stable

Unpredictable,
past, present and futures merge,
collapsing timelines

Cosmos in peril,
the tapestry unravells,
unmaking our world

Domino effect
God help us, what have we done?
History fading

Temporal cascade,
a schism in space and time,
the darkness rising

<u>Hotel Eidelon...</u>

A tragic day, or so they say
that brought their tragic curse.
Or was it night that saw their plight,
and spawned this chilling verse?
Where lovers dare to dance on air
to fate and murder foul.
But what's the cost when love is lost
and vengeance starts to prowl?

One stormy night, the lovers fight,
torrential rain that pours.
A broken car that brought them far
and lost to great outdoors.
A hotel sign of fate's design
as lightening breaks the storm.
So on they trod through mud and sod
to shelter, dry and warm.

Soaked to skin as they signed in,
then led unto their room.
Now warm and dry with anger spry,
their arguments resume.
But none foresaw the final straw
as he lashed out to strike,
that saw her fall without a call
upon the fire guard's pike.

'Oh God, she's dead' he meekly said,
his voice cracked with regret,
as so much blood began to flood,
a growing stain, claret.
Unto his knees, in prayer appease
"Take back this night I pray,
please let her live, my soul I give,
a cost I'll gladly pay"

So very odd, it was not God
who answered him that night.
For standing there in shadows bare,
a man with eyes alight.
"Do not fear for I am here
to raise her soul from death"
"Oh thank you Sir, my soul for her"
he said through ragged breath.

The man he laughed "Oh don't be daft,
I am not here for you.
It's she who called in death appalled
as you struck her askew.
Her dying need was rage to feed
beyond her final breath,
to bring such chills to those she kills,
like you who brought her death"

In death she's spawned, a woman scorned,
her fury raging on
and so she stood, from corpse no good,
the light within her gone.
Her loving kiss had seemed remiss
but drained his life-force bare.
Dead before he hit the floor,
his soul in bleak despair.

Now every year, the spirits stir
to mark that fateful night,
a crimson stain that speaks their pain
as they relive their plight.
Forever lost, so high the cost,
assures that guests won't sleep,
as shrieks and screams that haunt their dreams,
awake as spirits weep.

The Raven's Caw...

At dusk, pale sun dost set before
the twilight time that comes once more,
my foot falls echo sharp on stone
as harmonies of crickets drone,
behold the lonesome Raven's caw.

A shiver creeping up my spine,
a heart that pounds its beat with mine,
whispers fill the damping air
in swirls of fog on street so bare,
beware the lonesome Raven's sign.

As lamplight throws my shadow long
as madness grows in fear so strong,
as voices call beyond the grave,
as demons crawl on paths we crave,
bequeathed in lonesome Raven's song.

Moonlight fighting shadow's gloam,
footsteps leading swiftly home,
denying things my senses feel,
yet deep inside I know they're real,
the darkling lonesome Ravens roam

A glimpse that gleans an inner war
that knocks three times upon my door,
that finds me bound by candle light
to ward off spirits in the night,
I hear the lonesome Raven's caw.

So much in life I must atone,
such sins that haunt I can't condone,
the Raven's caw that speaks my doom,
my lamp that sways in shadow's gloom,
reveals the lonesome Raven's flown.

An omen that may spell my last,
a tell-tale heart that speaks the past,
this tapestry of life we weave,
so bound by chains of fate we leave,
such wings of lonesome Raven vast.

My footsteps loud on wooden floor,
I grip my head and plead 'No more'
The Raven's eyes so black and cold,
I pray and beg 'Let me grow old'
I hear the lonesome Raven's caw.

And quoth the Raven 'nev……..'

Well you know the rest…

<u>Murder Most Foul...</u>

As storm clouds rumbled overhead,
and thunder rages war,
as lightening strikes to break the calm
in rain's torrential pour.
Ironic that on such a night,
a predator should prowl
and bring us to the manor house
and to its murder foul.

A body in the library,
a knife stuck in his back,
Autumn, 1921,
as told by shameless hack.
Inspector Fritz is on the case,
the first upon the scene,
deducting from the evidence,
the secrets bared to glean.

"Ev'ning all, I guess you know
why you are gathered here,
for one of you has killed this night
but each has motive clear.
Lets look at all the facts so far
and narrow down our view
to catch the scoundrel in our midst
that caused us much ado.

The Victim had his many faults,
his marriage but a fake
to hide affairs with other men,
a poof, and no mistake.
That brings us to his widow fair,
a motive far from proud,
who even now recoils in shame
to hear these words aloud.

For if she left, he'd leave her broke,
no wealth or love to find,
but staying in a loveless sham
has caused her such a bind.
Alas, she has an alibi
that somewhat rules her out,
for cook has vouched her whereabouts
and left us little doubt.

Which brings us to his father's pride,
so dented by his shame,
his son, a whoopsie, Nancy boy,
whose mother is to blame.
His heart has grown so full of hate,
displayed in cold despise,
but would he kill his only son,
his heir with sinful lies?

No, he is no murderer,
he sat with his dear wife,
bed bound with malaria
and fighting for her life.
He too has an alibi,
removing him from blame,
abound the whispered rumours fly
that taint his family name.

Which brings us to the gardener,
who punched his puckered star
and taught him joys of Godless love,
disgraced, he fell so far.
Could it be a jealous spat,
a quarrel bound in death?
Did he reject you for his wife
and bring his final breath?

I know you have an alibi,
but we knew all along,
in Britain, 1921,
your deeds are very wrong
Higgins, cuff the bounder up
and clout him round the ear,
teach him that his heathen ways
are not permitted here."

"If I may" the Butler said.
"The deed was done by me,
for all the reasons you have said
that shame his family.
His mother taken to her bed,
his father in such pain,
his wife despairing of her life,
I had to break the chain.

I've lived and worked within this house,
since I was but a boy
and watched it thrive with so much love
of which he would destroy.
They've always been so good to me
and so it broke my heart
to see the life he chose to lead
was tearing them apart.

But also for another deed,
a debt from long time hence,
you see a wager had been sealed,
he owed me fifty pence.
Deceit is not the British way
and wagers must be paid
and secrets kept for honour's sake,
not openly displayed.

And so I took it on myself,
restore the family name,
a bad apple will rot the cart
and drive them all to shame.
So sad that it should come to this,
an act that I deplore
and so I throw myself upon
the mercy of the law"

"Okay Higgins, cuff him up,
that's two for hangman's rope,
that's all the mercy they will find,
I doubt they have a hope.
The butler did it, what a twist!
A man you'd overlook,
I've never known the like before,
someone should write a book"

And so concludes the murder case
upon that ghastly night
that brought us to the manor house
to freeze our blood in fright.
So many secrets to unfold
and yet more tales to tell
of murder foul and motives bound
in hearts where secrets dwell.

Blind Passion...

In cold despise I took her eyes
and fed her to the night.
I watched her call and blindly fall
and pray to see the light.

I took her shoes, my wanton muse,
tonight I must surpass.
And so I stalk the paths she'll walk,
hot coals or broken glass?

So many fears cocooned in tears
that find they have a voice
that rise inside when sight's denied
that brings about her choice.

And so she limps, I smile and glimpse,
her path of broken glass.
To see her feel a pain so real,
determined she must pass.

Her broken feet become my treat,
she trips to hands and knees.
With crimson trails, she sobs and wails
for mercy in her pleas.

Her will is gone, I'm so turned on
but I know I must wait.
Exquisite pain and half insane,
a lust that I must sate.

Her beauty rare, I grab her hair
and drag her through the shards.
Her tearing flesh so soft and fresh,
receive my kind regards.

At my command, I make her stand
and wait the killing blow.
I kiss her lips and grip her hips,
such beauty in her woe.

Is it wrong to lust and long
and do the things I do?
For all I crave, the pain I gave,
I whisper 'I love you'

A Death Of Ages...

I stood before the old priory ruins, pushing back the vegetation that grew from the cracks in the wall, so run down and in disrepair. I shook my head and wiped a tear from my eye at the dilapidation and neglect that had brought forth this fate upon this once magnificent place of worship. It had withstood numerous wars, it had offered shelter and sanctuary to many in times of hardship and so I vowed that I would come here every year to light a candle in vigil, offering a prayer in the old chapel in remembrance of darker times.

It was here that it all began for me so very long ago, Caldey Island in West Wales, just off the Tenby coast in the year of our lord, 1064. I was a mercenary, I'd kill for whoever paid the most for my services but with the invasion of Normandy, myself and my cohorts were driven inland and so we fled to that fateful island. Hauled up in the monastery where we had laid siege, slaughtering and torturing monks who would not comply to our demands. Delivering death and suffering in such great and creative abundance.

The remembrance of my actions shames me greatly, I was such an evil bastard back then. I would take such great joy and pride in the pain and fear that I brought to others. Men, women, even children, I cared not who... A thrill that would race my heart as I looked into their eyes at the moment that their minds became broken, I saw it so many, many times... I'd bring their loved ones to such heights of torment with such glee in my heart, boiling oil to pour on their naked backs, breaking their bones and shattering their teeth, gouging out their eyeballs as they wept for mercy.

And the shock in their eyes as their lives ebbed to naught by my hand, my blade thrust and twisted in their gut when they were too broken to bring that thrill any longer. And I would watch them die, agonized to extremity for hours on end... I have so much blood on my hands, it makes me cry...

I stood in the priory when it was new, bathed in the blood of the innocent, my very presence, an affront to God. And in the prayers of all who had sought shelter and sanctuary, I was bestowed my path to salvation in an act of divine intervention. For the Archangel descended in tribulation of my sins, burning my soul in a fire of purity, stripping away my sins to an innocence of heart. My cohorts, cast to the depths of Hell to burn in the inferno for an eternity of torment, their souls blackened beyond redemption.

So I asked unto the Archangel 'Why wouldst thou spare'th me? I am a monster' and he said unto me 'Thy heart be heavy, burdened by cruelty born of cruelty. I offer unto thee a path of salvation that thou may redeem'eth thy soul in the eyes of God'
'What wouldst thou hath me do?'
'Thou wouldst be an Angel of death, that thou may reap'eth the souls of the dying. Thou wouldst leadeth the pure of heart to the gates of Heaven as thou wouldst cast the unworthy to the pit of eternal damnation'

I dropped to my knees with such sorrow and regret in my heart, head bowed as tears of remorse stung my cheeks in their flow. The Archangel reached unto me and as I looked upon him, he wiped away my tears and baptized me in their purity.

'Thou shalt walk among the living in knowledge of the dying in an eternal pilgrimage of redemption. Thou shalt not deviate from thy path, nor bow to temptation in penance of thy sins. I anoint thee, Angel of death... Now stand and walketh thy path...' And so he was gone.

All around me, my victims both dead and dying looked unto me to guide them from this life and so I embraced them in my first act of servitude to the lord. But I could not apologise to them, how could I? Somehow, sorry just seemed way too small a gesture for my actions, yet each of them kissed me upon my cheek and forgave me my trespasses and I was humbled in their forgiveness. Truly, I was touched to tears and so my path became clear.

Now here I stand, nearly one thousand years later, holding a candle of hope in a prayer to humanity. My true purpose, known only to the pure of heart, embraced by the ever vigilant monks of Caldey Island Monastery, in annual welcome as they break bread and feed me. They cleanse my heart as they pray for my immortal soul, bound to eternal servitude as they wait with each passing year for my return. That one day they may lay me to rest when finally my penance is paid and my pilgrimage at an end...

And truly, though I know the path to eternal rest, I decree that its price is too high, for if arrogance would allow me forgiveness of self, then my salvation would be in vain and my divine task would be for naught... And so I shall forever walk this path, guiding the lost souls and crying hearts from this life to find their place in eternity...

Dark Confessions:
A Christmas Special...

I've always been so very careful... Covering my tracks, leaving no loose ends for others to stumble across my work... Clearing the scene of anything that could lead the authorities to my door... I've made an art form of juggling my night time activities with my daytime life... How the fuck was there a witness? Maybe the police are using the media to try and rattle me, get me to make a mistake, that's got to be it... I don't make mistakes, I survey, I stalk and I plan before I even think of making my move. I even account for variables and deviations, there's no way there could have been a witness, they're fucking with me... They have to be...

Like most serial killers, I have my rituals and routines and no doubt my fair share of delusional beliefs that help me justify my actions in the bigger picture, yadder, yadder, yadder, bing, bang boff... I can't even keep a straight face spouting that bullshit... It is what is, I'm a fucking hero... I'm an artist... I don't give a toss about M.O.'s, Modus Operandi, Methods of Operation or any of the other crap they try to spoon feed you in crime dramas and CSI bollocks...

Hi, my name is Donnie and yeah, I've had my share of Donnie Darko jokes but I'm cool with that, I loved the movie. Just not Donald, never Donald, coz that makes me sound like a twat, thank you mum and dad. As you can imagine, I had my fair share of Donald Duck to Donald Fuck to Fuckwit to fucking weirdo throughout my school life. Not the most inspired progression, I grant you but when dealing with under achieving primates, it's hard to picture anything with any great wit.

My father was a wife beater, speed/meth addict and a notorious drunk, a real piece of work. We had social services calling twice a week and when things really got out of hand, the police would be banging on the door with complaints of domestic disturbance.

Yep, sweet childhood huh? Topped only by that one defining Christmas when I trotted eagerly down the stairs to see if Santa had left me that Playstation I'd so dearly hoped and wished for. I'd dropped enough hints to sink a fucking ship. But the surprise I'd received was a lot more devastating than I could have ever dreamed of.

He'd finally gone too far, he'd cracked her over the head with his whisky bottle, fracturing her scull before she'd smacked it on the corner of the mantle in her fall and he just fell asleep in the chair as she'd slowly died of the head injuries and progressive loss of blood. Happy fucking Christmas!!! I'd watched them cart her away on a gurney with a blanket pulled up over her face, so surreal in the flashing blue lights, the house a hive of slow motion activity as my father was handcuffed and taken away fighting, the crackle and blarb of police and ambulance radios... And I remember someone putting a blanket around my shoulders as they led me from the house to a waiting car... I was absolutely devastated... And if I'm completely honest, it was probably the last time I ever really truly felt anything... And little did I know that this would be the catalyst for who I would become.

After that I'd stayed with my aunty but she quickly decided she couldn't cope with me, I think I cramped her style, the selfish cow. And so I was moved around from foster home to foster home, a number in the system, the traumatised little boy that nobody wanted. I began killing animals in an effort to feel something but nothing came and I got good at it. And after once being caught, I quickly learned how to cover my tracks and again I got good at it...

It wasn't until I was fifteen that I killed my first human and God I felt so alive... Basically, a chav had pulled a knife on me, wrong place, wrong time, wrong man... I'd waited for him to thrust, gripped his wrist and held it in both my hands as he desperately tried to pull it back toward him. I then used his own momentum and pushed, using his upward pull to direct the blade to his throat.

The shock on his face had been priceless, dropping to his knees as his windpipe gurgled around the blade before he slumped forward, driving the blade home to his death as it tore through the vertebrae in his neck. But it had all happened so fast, that there was nothing to savour and I knew I wanted more... God, I wanted more... The thrill of the kill... The power it had made me feel was so intoxicating that it was almost sexual in its nature and I began craving it like nothing before in my life... It was like a moment of clarity, I'd found my purpose...

As time went on, so the craving became so much stronger, and I knew I'd have to be careful... I felt like an addict slaved to my vice...

There's not much that gets to me, but after my childhood experiences, I have a real rage that rises in the wake of men beating on women. And so this became my focus as first I began taking out pimps in the less savoury, less policed parts of the city. And again, nothing too grandiose, just tailed them, waited for my opportunity and stepped up behind them, swiftly slitting their throats and watching them bleed like the pigs that they are as their eyes bulged and tongues protruded as warm life-blood pumped over their hands as they desperately grasped at their throats. You see, I'm not a monster, I choose my victims well... Sadly it wasn't long before the police had worked out my pattern as new prostitutes had begun appearing on the street corners. I stalked a few of them to see if my instincts had been right and wasn't at all surprised to find them making reports to plain clothed operatives in law enforcement. I knew then that it was time to slow down and reign in these urges before they consumed me and I fucked up.

Eighteen months had passed by in the interim and I'd successfully kept a lid on these dark cravings. Until eventually news had reached me via my aunty that my dad would soon be released from prison, having served his sentence for the events of that fateful night. Like I said before, I don't feel much in the way of emotion, I have to fake it for the most part to blend in. But that night, I had a wave of devastating emotion wash over me as I relived the night my mum died in an idol, reflective fantasy, born of remembrance.

97

And I cried, weeping like the child I left behind on that fateful night... And I knew I had to make him pay for what he had done to me... For what he'd done to my mum... What he had made me become... And so I planned and schemed of how this was going to go down, forgiveness was never an option, I really couldn't let it go... I needed closure...

And so I began to buy in supplies; bleach, plastic sheeting, industrial packing tape, a rubber diving suit, latex gloves, cooking knives, tons of cheap clothes from charity shops and a number of free syringes from the local methadone clinic... God bless the heroin addicts... I then started scoping abandoned warehouses and properties that wouldn't draw attention until I found one perfect for my needs... Secluded and clearly untouched for a number of years, just on the outskirts of the city and ironically, an abandoned abattoir...

Upon his release, I stalked him for a few months and got to know his routines and hang outs... No surprises that he'd find his way to pubs and bars before finding a taste for prostitutes and bar skanks. Then to discover he was one of those men who needed to choke women to sustain his errection, the man just sickened me... My childhood memories of his lifestyle had always put me off touching the booze, I never wanted to end up like him, ever...

Finally when I was near enough ready to go, I shaved my head and waxed my body... After all, loose, stray hairs have a nasty habit of dropping you in the shit in terms of evidence at crime scenes. And so I was set and found my way to the point where our paths would converge and waited for him to pass by. It was almost too easy and I was angry with him for not being more of a challenge, for not putting up more of a struggle... I hit him once and he was unconscious, damn him... He frightened the life out of me when I was a child, yet now this frail old piss-head just disgusted me... Repulsed me in his weakness... Where was the fire? Where was the rage that had so terrified me and scarred me as a child? He would pay for that too...

Having reached the abattoir, I stripped to my under-ware and donned the skin tight diving suit and put on my latex gloves. I then laid out a large square of plastic sheeting, stripped him and laid him out on it, using the industrial packing tape to secure his arms and taping his wrists together behind his back. I then taped his ankles and then his knees together to restrict his movement, before slapping him about to wake him up.

His eyes suddenly snapped open, quickly widening as he began to take in his surroundings and finally realisation dawned as he contemplated his situation. A delightfully, delicious 'Oh Crap' moment that will stay with me forever and made me grin widely.
'Where am I? Who are you?' he asked with a tremble in his voice.
'Do you not recognise your own son, Father?' I replied calmly.
'Donnie? Is that you?'
'Come now Father, surely you can't have forgotten me already'
'I never forgot you Donnie… I am so sorry about everything'

Suddenly rage coursed through me and impulsively I sprang forward and punched him hard in the mouth, his front teeth breaking with the impact of the blow as his mouth filled with blood and he began coughing and spluttering crimson tooth fragments. 'YOU DON'T GET TO BE SORRY…' I bellowed at him in fury, before stepping back and turning away from him to compose myself. I took a few deep breaths in an effort to calm myself down. It was then that I noticed the sting in my knuckles and found that his broken teeth had torn through the glove and cut me. I winced and breathed deeply to suppress the rage. I was getting emotional and that was not a good sign. I needed to get myself in check before continuing or I would make a mistake and implicate myself.

You see, the plan had been to calmly break him down over a few hours until he'd reached regret and then kill him, but he was not giving me the satisfaction and closure that I needed. I couldn't trust myself not to react emotionally. Like I said before, I haven't felt anything since that night, I've been so numb for so very long and now emotions were sweeping over me like a tsunami and I really didn't know how to deal with them. I knew I was going to have to cut this short before I did something stupid.

I wanted him to suffer, that was a given… I wanted to really hurt him but I couldn't trust my own judgement enough to know when to stop. I was going to have to improvise…

I had initially brought the syringe to blow an air bubble into a vein that he may go peacefully after finding remorse for killing my mum. I'm not an animal…
And I'd brought the bleach to clean up any potential evidence in the aftermath of the deed. But now I'd fucked up big time and broken his teeth and despite the thrill of his sobs, I knew that death would be deemed as suspicious, so I couldn't risk throwing caution to the wind. I would simply make him suffer and watch him die.
So I quickly ripped off some tape and covered his mouth, then finding the syringe among my belonging, I used it to suck up a full vial of bleach and injected it directly into a juicy vein in his arm and sat back to watch the show.

I was actually pretty good at biology and chemistry at school, so I was intrigued to see the effects as I ran the theory through my head. It was fascinating and thankfully sated my baser urges to cut him and beat him to a pulp. The extreme pain was almost immediate and his face reddened as his arm began to blister as his agonised screams were muffled through the tape. He looked at me pleadingly through the devastation of the blood vessel as clots formed and travelled to begin blocking and systematically shutting down his vital organs over a number of hours. He writhed like a fish out of water until the shaking began, at which point, I crossed to him and held up his head to look into his eyes. 'Goodbye Father…' I said softly and kissed his forehead, before holding him in my arms tightly until finally, the shaking stopped. I wept quietly at first, then sobs turned to roars and I actually felt better after a good cry as I began putting the past behind me and moving on.

That was five years ago, I'm a lot more in control now and have my cravings bridled to necessity. I just kill once a year, it's like my Christmas treat in remembrance of my mother and father. The media have named me 'Santa Claws' which amuses me greatly…

Today's front page headline reads **'Santa Claws Strikes Again'** in reference to the guy I took out this year. It has this wonderful cartoon image of a rabid Santa beside the story… LMAO!!!

Basically he was a deadbeat husband who frequently knocked the shit out of his wife after a few too many drinks. Sound familiar? Okay I've got an M.O., so sue me… I started tailing him in September, even stopped to chat with him on occasion. The guy was scum, no regrets, no remorse and couldn't see a thing wrong with his life. Volatile, violent and embraced as a way of life that old joke:

Q. What do you call a woman with two black eyes?
A. Not listening the first time.

I figured 'Yep, he's our man alright' and set about this year's treat. Like I say, I'd been trailing him since September and I was peeved to realise they were already playing Christmas carols in the shops. His poor wife was taking a regular beating and living in fear of her life, with police and social services regularly visiting the troubled house. But sadly powerless under the law to actually do anything until she pressed charges that in turn formed a vicious circle in that she was too afraid to because of the threats of what he might do.

I took him a day before Christmas Eve, spiked his drink with a mild sedative to slow his reflexes and waited along his route home. It wasn't long before I saw him lumbering up the road like some tired beast of burden, stooping occasionally to rest before moving on. I simply waited until the street was completely empty, drove up beside him and offered a lift home. He climbed in willingly and slumped in the seat with his eyes closed. Perfect!

I then swiftly drove on to the abattoir. And I still can't believe the police haven't thought to check there in previous years, maybe it's too obvious or so long unused that no one even thinks of it. Either way it suits me fine, I'm not complaining… It's all good…
I helped him out of the car and brought him inside to the main area, allowing him to drop onto the waiting plastic sheeting as I quickly changed into my diving suit and donned a Santa coat and hat. What can I say? I'm a sucker for media portrayal and front page coverage. They create a myth, so I've got to live up to it…

I then began stripping him and taping his wrists together. And though he let out a few disgruntled snorts, he didn't actually begin to stir until I'd strapped his ankles into the overhead shackles they used for pig slaughter and hoisted him into the air as the blood rushed to his head.

Killed like a pig, I love life's ironies…

'What the fuck?' he cried out.

'Good evening Mr Johnson' I replied with crisp, bank manager sincerity.

'Get me the fuck down!!! I'll fucking kill you!!!' he roared.

'Not really much of a motivation, is it now, Mr Johnson?'

'What do you want?'

'Ah, straight to the nub of the matter, good for you Sir… I'm afraid you've been a very naughty boy, haven't you?'

'WHAT???'

'I'm afraid you made Santa's naughty list, Mr Johnson' I said calmly with a mock jutting lip.

'You'd better get me the fuck down, right now'

'As much as I respect your bold, can do attitude, I'm afraid I must decline. You see we have a few urgent matters to discuss in regard to your continual spousal abuse'

'Fuck you, I've got rights'

'I'm afraid you've forfeited them Mr Johnson, the only rights you hold right now is your right to make peace with the world'

'WHAT? I don't understand'

'Evidently so, but just to clarify, you are not long to remain in this world… You will die tonight… And I don't mean that maliciously, it is simply a fact… The world is better off without you…'

'But you can't, that's… That means you're…'

'Ah realisation dawns… That's right Mr Johnson, I'm that Santa… You see, I have no qualms about hurting you and your screams will be like some divine symphony to my ears'

'Someone will hear me'

'I'm afraid not, there's nobody for miles'

'People will notice I'm gone'

'And so they will rejoice'

'They will find me'

'I'm afraid they'll not even miss you, nobody likes you, in fact, most say you're an asshole' I said in a mock conspiracy tone with a stage whisper, theatrical gesture.
'Someone will come'
'Who? Please tell me, Mr Johnson. Who will come?'
'I don't know...'
'Exactly, I think we're done with denial now, don't you Mr Johnson. Let's just get on with the business at hand'
'You can't do this...' he said with an edge of panic in his voice.
'Oh I think you'll find I can' I smiled as I took out a small knife, knelt beside him and stabbed it sharply between two ribs in the right side of his chest and gyrated the blade a number of times. 'Do you believe me now, Mr Johnson?' I asked in the same calm, levelled voice as he froze and gasped as the blade slid in, grimacing as it twisted, then minor relief as I pulled it out. 'Well?' I pressed 'Do you believe me now?'

He nodded vigorously, fear creasing his face as his tears ran down his forehead.
'Jolly good, we're getting somewhere then... So tell me a bit about your better half, Mr Johnson, why do you beat her?'
'I'm sorry...' he sobbed.
'Uh uuuh' I mock buzzered 'Wrong answer' I replied and pushed my finger into his knife wound, between his ribs and began to wiggle it about as he howled the place down.
'You know, I could do this all night but I'm afraid I've got a schedule to keep, can we skip to your protestations and get straight to the remorse'
'Schedule?'
'What? You think just because I'm a serial killer, I don't have Christmas plans? Really Mr Johnson, that's blatant stereotyping and if not for the timing, we'd most assuredly be discussing that too'
'Why are you doing this?' he sobbed.
'It's quite simple... I'm making my list and checking it twice... Well you know the rest...'
'I'm begging you... oh please don't kill me'
'Tra la la la, la la la la... You know the modern connotations of that song amuse me greatly'

'You're insane'

'No honestly, hear me out... There's that line 'Gladly don your gay apparel?' Do you realise that in this day and age, it asks you to wear your skimpiest vest, designer shades and tightest jeans in December. Now that is madness'

'Please, stop this'

'You're quite right Mr Johnson, it shames me to admit that I'm stereotyping now. But don't worry, you can rest assured that I'll work on it' I smiled as I brought up the blade and held it to his throat as his face contorted in terror. 'I'm afraid we're wasting time Mr Johnson'

'NO'

'You'll notice that below you is the drain where slaughter blood is washed away, convenient huh?' I said, gesturing the taped hole in the plastic sheeting.

'Please, don't do this'

'Goodbye Mr Johnson and Merry Christmas' I smiled as I brought the blade swiftly across his throat and quickly stepped back as he bucked like a fish on a line as his blood pumped from his neck, over his face, filling his mouth and nose, before being swallowed by the waiting drain's hungry mouth.

Some time later when he'd finished dripping and twitching, I lowered him down onto the plastic sheeting and slitting him from groin to chest, quickly set about removing his organs as I hollowed out his shell like a pumpkin. I then washed him and the organs thoroughly to lose the last remnants of blood before drying and dressing him in a cheap Santa suit. I then patted dry his organs and intestines and hung them up to dry a little more and so the day wore on.

At around 6pm, I briefly borrowed his house keys, headed over to his house in the car. I waited for his wife to retreat to the kitchen at the back of the house, quietly let myself in and crept along the hallway, quickly ducking into the dining room as she came out of the kitchen and went into the toilet.

Seeing my chance, I swiftly headed to the kitchen to see a freshly made cup of tea and spiked it with some sedative to help her sleep as I prepared her Christmas morning surprise. I could feel my excitement building; it made me feel like a kid again.

After quietly letting myself out, I headed back to the abattoir, parked up and nipped in to pick him up, bring him out to the car, put him in the passenger seat and put on his seatbelt to hold him steady... After all, safety first... I then nipped back in, collected all the organs and bagged them up in towels before putting them into refuse sacks and loading them into the boot of the car. I then went back in for the third and final time to clean up and remove any and all traces of my presence and my activities therein. Then bagging up the plastic sheeting and various other paraphernalia, I placed it on the back seat with intention to burn later. Finally, I was able to jump into the driving seat and we were away.

Twenty minutes later, I pulled up outside his house and peeped through the living room window to see her crashed out for the count on the sofa... Aww sweet... So I quickly let myself in and carried her to bed, gently laying her down and putting the duvet over her as she slept on obliviously. Next I nipped out and got him in from the car, bringing him into the house and sitting him in the armchair in the living room, holding a big card that said "Merry Christmas"

Then nipping back out the car again, I got the organs from the boot and brought them into the house, decorating the tree festively with them. His intestines looping around and spiralling it with various organs draped on the branches for balance. Ironic that this was the origin of tree decoration in a Druid sacrifice on Winter Solstice for health and prosperity, so keenly adapted by Christianity for Christmas with tinsel and baubles...

But enough of my rambling, I stood back and surveyed my work proudly. Yes, she'll appreciate this after the initial shock... Maybe not today, but tomorrow she can play the devastated, grieving widow and in time, she can learn to live again... And one day, she may even feel gratitude... My work here is done...

...Until next year of course...

For your amusement...

How I like my Women...

I like my women like
I like my cars,
built for speed,
comfort and endurance,
minimal noise,
no annoying squeaks,
grumbles or groans,
reliable, no breakdowns,
no roadside drama,
great body work,
minimal paint job,
gear box
that can take a grinding,
adjustable seating,
turns on easy
and drives like a dream,
when I gun her engine,
I want her to purr
like a kitten,
reacts when I push
the right buttons,
strong back bumper
for collision and impact,
a soft voice to direct me
on life's road
and the bonus feature
of built in air bags
to bury my face in…

Sadly, like my cars,
I always seem to end up
with insurance write offs…

Misconstrued...

Things they seem to escalate
when words are misconstrued,
when things are said in innocence
that others take as rude.
Just the other day I saw
my neighbor fill her car
with all the junk from round her house
for scrap-yard au revoir.

I hadn't seen her headphones worn
until it was too late.
Removing one to hear me speak,
I smiled with manly gait.
Her shock was clear for all she'd heard,
the words that left me sunk.
Were simply 'I would love to put
my junk into your trunk'

Her knee jerked up to meet my groin,
and then she slapped me silly,
in hindsight now I realize,
she thought I meant my willy!
I figured I'd apologize,
it's not what she'd assumed,
my words had been in innocence
but still they left me doomed.

For as I stood I tripped the curb,
my footing lost its rests,
face first to her cleavage launched,
my hands had grabbed her breasts,
then slipping down to hips and ass
to steady as I stood.
Embarrassed I apologized,
alas it did no good.

Horrified she'd grabbed her can
of triple strength bear mace.
And sprayed and sprayed and sprayed and sprayed
it all into my face.
And so I started vomiting,
my eyes they burned with tears,
trying to explain to her,
its not how it appears.

She kicked and kicked and kicked and kicked,
I thought she'd never stop,
so thankful someone witnessed it
and thought to call a cop.
I lay there handcuffed to a bed
in hospital subdued
because my words in innocence
were badly misconstrued.

Bruised and battered, blurry eyed
with morphine kicking in,
that seemed to gently ease away
the aches and pains within.
My balls the size of coconuts,
a pain you can't surpass,
until they surgically remove
her shoe wedged in my ass.

I guess the lesson I have learned
is watch the words you say,
if things begin to escalate,
its time to walk away.
Apologize when things calm down
and tempers are less frayed
before you're facing prison time
for dumb mistakes you've made.

Homo-Erectus...

I bet the title made you look
and made you glance it twice.
It doesn't mean what you'd assume
or thoughts it might entice.
It's not a game or boast or cry
or medical condition.
Its not a gay and horny guy
demanding your submission.

I kinda knew it had to be
of pre-historic themes,
although I thought of cave drawn porn
with gay and lavish schemes.
And then I thought the strangest thing,
a caveman with a boner,
then a hunk construction kit
and huge gay night club owner.

Disturbing thoughts I hear you say,
alas I do agree,
such tangents for my mind to doubt
my sexuality.
If so, the closet's very big,
too deep to just come out,
I must be stood in Narnia
and too far back to shout.

But I know its not the case,
I feel the primal calls.
I crave a woman's gentle touch,
not hairy arse and balls.
In truth its probably the weed
that led me down these paths.
I never liked YMCA
or appletini baths.

I've strayed right off my train of thought,
I know I had a point.
But this happens every time
I deign to smoke a joint.
Giggles, munchies, strangest thoughts
that stem from but a word
and so I find so much to write
where wisdom meets absurd.

Now where was I? It's hard to tell.
I've got it now I think.
Homo-Erectus, upright ape,
to man, a missing link.
Okay children, don't look shocked,
just work on your essay.
Evolution is your prompt,
your topic for today.

Duuuuude, I'm sooooo high right now… ☺

My Visit with Grandma...

The other day I saw my Gran,
we chatted over tea,
speaking of the family
and how our lives should be.
Talking 'til the cows come home,
we put the world to rights,
brewing yet another pot
of tea with cookie bites.

Conversations, revelations,
tales of in her day,
working hard and cleaning house,
then off to church to pray.
How the world had changed so much,
with rations after war,
children raised in poverty,
yet wholesome to the core.

'Men today are impolite,
not like they used to be,
they'd take your coat or hold the door,
enjoy your company'
I sighed because I knew the truth,
but wondered should I dare.
You see I really love my Gran,
a truth I rarely share.

But Gran respects an honest tongue,
so what else could I do?
But speak my mind to let her know
the truth I thought I knew.
And so I took the deepest breath,
let out a deeper sigh,
and told her all the things I knew
were truths she can't deny.

'It's not that men are impolite,
to not hold coat or door.
The truth is men are not trying
to fuck you anymore.
Your face is like a crumpled sheet,
you smell of pee and shout,
your vaj looks like a dead hedgehog
whose guts are hanging out'

'Oh Grandma, what big eyes you have'
Her dentures hit the floor,
she hit me with her walking frame
and kicked me out the door.
Shouting such obscenities
as I ran up the street,
sadly we don't talk no more
as she declines to meet.

I wonder how things got so bad,
I only told the truth,
it's not like I said stinky gums
or single rotting tooth.
I'll work on my diplomacy
and do the best I can,
I really want to make things right,
I miss my dear old Gran...

F**king Delivery Men...

It mainly is the little things,
that stress us all to Hell,
like waiting for deliveries,
that leave us far from well.
"Make sure you're in from 9 to 5,
make sure you don't go out"
they leave us pacing up and down,
couped up, we want to shout.

They can't give a specific time?
It has to be their way?
I swear they get the cruelest thrill
from fucking up our day.
The fact we have to pay for this,
the service they provide,
has got to be the sickest joke
but still we must abide.

Afraid to nip off for a pee,
a need you must forstall.
God help you if you need to shit,
coz that's when they will call.
Holding out til touching cloth,
'til you can wait no more,
and dash into the loo to feel
a pain that makes you roar.

Unclenching buttocks, tight too long,
your situation dire,
'coz now you sing like Johnny Cash,
got you a ring of fire.
Crying, tears and face so red
such strain and pain complete
with teeth marks in the toilet door
and nail marks in the seat.

Trying hard to finish up
before the doorbell rings,
constipation kicks in hard
with all the pain it brings.
And just when you have turtle's head,
a knock sounds on the door,
announcing they have brought the goods
you ordered from the store.

But do they hang around for you
to finish, wipe and shout?
No, they leave a card to say,
they called and you were out.
Then they cop an attitude
when called as you complain,
they tell you stay in all next week,
they'll squeeze you in again.

It fucks me off, the way they work
and cause us such ordeals.
The other week, I took revenge
to show them how it feels.
I waited for the door to knock
and answered with a smile.
I made him wait and closed the door
and said I'd be a while.

I crept out through the garden door,
and opened up his truck,
climbed in and took the biggest dump
as bowels became unstuck.
And then crept back to let him know
its okay to proceed,
and followed him back to the truck,
completing my misdeed.

He climbed inside with wrinkled nose,
as I slammed both the doors
and locked the bastard up inside
with stench that one abhors.
He retched and puked and banged the doors
and claimed he can't survive.
Like Arnie I said 'I'll be back,
somewhere twixt nine and five'

My question for you Doctor Az,
now police have brought me here,
is who does your deliveries
and are their prices dear?
Can you prescribe a laxative
to make my movements quick?
Before something that I'll regret
is more than just slap-stick.

Who the F**k is Larry?

People tell me
'He's as happy as Larry'
I want to know who this Larry is…
Because when I find out,
I'm going to kick him
so hard in the bollocks,
then distribute an atomic wedgie
that will see the elastic
at the back
of his underwear
yank his head back
as I loop it over his forehead…

Why is he so fucking happy?
No one deserves to be that happy…

…Larry is going down…

Massage chairs & Motorway Services...

The motorway services,
the obligatory rush
to the loos,
...the mad dash
to the massage chairs...

While friends,
squirmed and moaned
in the quelling
of aches and pains,
I just felt something
tickling my arse...

If it starts
tickling my balls too,
we're in business,
but still no easing
of my stiff lower back...

So naturally I started
bouncing about
to get the thing working,
still nothing...

So I stood to see
what the problem was
and was stunned
to discover
a poor old man
who'd fallen asleep
there earlier...

My Lesson:

Always look over my shoulder before I sit...

The Bus of the Damned...

I woke because my room's too hot,
awake by half past six,
I curse the lack of sleep I got
and slurp my caffeine fix.
86 degrees outside,
and that's just in the shade.
The grass is brown, the plants have died,
and skin feels like its flayed.

I caught the bus to hit the shop,
still early, my dismay,
the bus pulled up at every stop,
OH GOD, its pension day.
Like living dead, they shuffled on,
it must be their rush hour.
So soon I know that hope is gone,
as perfumes overpower.

Lavender and talc and pee,
makes for a sickly blend,
that makes me gag and want to flee,
before I meet my end.
Hearing aids that screech so loud
and pierce both my ears,
then someone crapped amidst the crowd
and brought my eyes to tears.

Walking frames and sticks and canes,
that stamp my feet and toes.
So deaf they shout as each complains,
of ailments they disclose.
None can hear the other speak,
which makes them louder still,
repeating every word they shriek
and moan they feel a chill.

Windows closed because they're cold,
it's 86 degrees,
I bite my tongue because their old
and pray for gentle breeze.
But all I taste is waft of arse
that blends with body sweat,
perfumes masking smells that pass,
all sides I am beset.

Thankfully I see my stop
and push the waiting bell,
salvation at the open shop
to lead me from this Hell.
But I cannot reach the door,
for old folks in my way,
the driver calls out 'Anymore,
please leave without delay'.

I shout to tell the driver 'WAIT!
I need to get off here'
But old folks shout to seal my fate
that makes my calls unclear.
Shouting they don't need this stop,
as doors shut with a wheeze,
the bus pulls off, I'm stuck atop
in 86 degrees…

NOOOOOOOOOoooOOO!!!

NOOOOOOOOOOOoooOO!!!

…Wind rushing through my hair…

…The streets like a google map…

…How did it come to this???

…I remember hearing people
screaming… Pointing…

'HE'S GOING TO JUMP!!!'

…Now I find myself
hurtling toward
the ground…

And I know
I should
be terrified,
I should be fretting
about everyone
I'll leave behind,
all the things
I never
got around to
but wanted to
before I died…

DIED???

…All I can think
is that any
minute now,
I'm going
to be
a pavement
pizza with everything…

...And really,
I wouldn't mind
so much,
but I
was
trying
to talk
the bastard down...

<u>Raging RDWRER...</u>

The Bastard cut my up...
...Sorry but I couldn't let that go...

Well of course
I had to let him know
he'd royally pissed me off
and in hindsight
it might have appeared
a bit extreme
to follow him 250 miles,
run him off the road
and threaten
to ram his teeth
so far down his throat,
he'd need to stick
his toothbrush
up his arse
to clean them...

...Sorry Officer, it won't happen again...

Happy Birthday Beth!!!

Hey there Beth, was passing by
and thought I might pop in.
Balloons and banners caught my eye
and brought a massive grin.
I've brought the ice-cream and the cake,
oh boy, we'll have such fun,
and roll around the mess we'll make
before the day is done.

I daydream for a little while
of showers, fun and games
that swells a bulge to raise a smile
and call you naughty names.
Lost in dreams of bubble bath
in pampered thoughts defined
but Rosco charges up the path
with Helen close behind.

The trolls so full of energy
and work as such a team,
too late I see them charge at me
and end my naughty dream.
Rosco leaps, his paws outstretched
and cracks me in the balls,
such pain and so I cried and retched
amidst my high pitched squalls.

Blacking out, I stagger back
and that's where Helen waits,
behind my legs that go so slack,
a new pain now translates.
Impaled upon a garden gnome,
I crawl along the grass
in agony to reach your home,
a gnome stuck up my ass.

I reach your porch where journals glance
and knock upon your door
'Oh Beth, please call an ambulance,
forgive my girlish roar…
Just one thing…' I weep to you
with staggered, sobbing breath
'the thing I'm here to bid you most
is Happy Birthday Beth!!!'

<u>Curiosity...</u>

I'm that guy with the light-bulb
stuck up my arse
and its not because
my colon had a great idea
or that I need to see when my head
is firmly wedged up there,
nor that I fell on it awkwardly
or any of the excuses I repeatedly use…

Truth is, I get bored easily,
boredom leads to curiosity
and curiosity leads
to embarrassing trips
to the hospital…

…Still, I'm way ahead of the cat
in terms of consequence to curiosity…

<u>Stoned Thoughts, sexy secrets and</u> <u>Random Rambles...</u>

Pull three papers from wrap... **It always amazes me, the crazy thoughts and tangents my mind visits when I have a smoke...** *Line papers up... Lick... Stick...* **Like if L'Oréal is making eyelashes look three times longer, why are they not making condoms?** *Add bacci... Spread bacci...* **And where do you draw the line between art and pornography?** *Strike lighter... Hold blim aloft...* **I guess if you rub your chin thoughtfully and get a twitch in the trouser region, it constitutes art...** *Burn... Sprinkle liberally... Roll...* **but if you actually get your penis out and beat it to death, it must be porn...** *Add roach... Put to lips... Light...* **And in this age of apparent equality, it's okay for a woman to brutally and quite rudely refuse a man's sexual advances...** *Inhale deeply... Exhale slowly...* **But when a woman is rejected, it's a capital offence... When once being hit upon I politely said "You're clocking up some serious mileage on your vajometer and I've got more self respect than to sleep with you", and I'm the bad guy???** *Oh God YES, that hit the spot...* **And what's the deal with dirty talk? "Call me naughty" "Tell me I'm a dirty girl" yet when you improvise and tell her "You're a stinking, filthy, disease ridden whore", she cries long and loud... I just don't get it... It must be something to do with intonation...** *Inhale deeply... Exhale slowly...* **And am I the only guy who's never met a woman who can give a decent blow-job? Grinding it between her teeth like she's skipped breakfast and lunch and hit the all you can eat buffet hard...** *Inhale deeply... Exhale slowly...* **Then apparently I killed the mood when she said 'fuck me up the arse' coz I declined and warned her of the dangers of rectal** cancer from having me white wash her kidneys while crashing the tradesman's entrance and thumping her up the back passage... *Tap ash into the ashtray...* I mean don't get me wrong, each to their own, but I've seen what comes out of my own arse and if she thinks I would want to put my dick into that, she's sorely mistaken... I'm the one who should be offended yet she's the one in tears... AGAIN!!! I really don't get it... *Inhale deeply... Exhale slowly...* Like most men, I like strong, independent women but where do you make the distinction between a strong, independent woman and a selfish, stroppy strumpet with a bad attitude and extreme rage issues? *Inhale deeply... Exhale slowly...* Where do you draw the line? Is it when you sign that dotted line of contractual prostitution that we call marriage? *Tap ash into the ashtray...* Or when you hold that gun in your mouth, praying to God that today is the day that you'll have the balls to actually pull the trigger and go through with it? *Inhale deeply... Exhale slowly...* And am I the only guy in the free world who washes his hands after visiting the toilet??? I remember this guy rolling his eyes at me before promptly mauling all the buffet food at a dinner party, it sickened me... *Inhale deeply... Exhale slowly...* So I promptly walked up to him and asked if he likes the smell of bollocks on his hands as he eats, right before I stirred his beer with my penis... And although I left in an ambulance, I think it was a point well made... *Inhale deeply... Exhale slowly...* And if the pen is mightier than the sword, why is it but a typo away from the penis, mightier than the sword? But then again, I have always considered myself one of the finest pork swordsmen in all of England... *Inhale deeply... Exhale slowly... Stub out in ashtray...* Touché away...

<u>More Stoned Thoughts</u>
<u>and Random Rambles...</u>

Pull three papers from wrap... **It starts with a tooth brush left in the bathroom for sleepovers, innocent enough it might seem, but don't be fooled,** *Line papers up... Lick... Stick...* **then it escalates to one of your bedroom drawers gradually filling with her stuff which in time spills over into the bedroom as cushions and drapes begin appear.** *Add bacci... Spread bacci...* **Next your bathroom will be full of beauty products, leg razors, bath salts, potions and spells,** *Strike lighter... Hold blim aloft...* **then finally you'll find the lock removed from the toilet door.** *Burn... Sprinkle liberally... Roll...* **A heinous crime, the last sanctuary of man,** *Lick... Stick...* **I mean back in the day, we had studies and libraries where we'd retreat to do our most profound thinking in a woman free environment.** *Add roach... Put to lips... Light...* **Alas, those days are far behind us, so we adapt and the toilet becomes the place we retreat to crap, wank, think and read.** *Inhale deeply... Exhale slowly...* **So what gives them the right to remove our locks and stroll in, demanding a courtesy flush,** *Oh God YES, that hit the spot...* **choking us as they brandish air-freshener, yapping at us with no regard for the sacred unwritten law as they breach our sanctuaries during what should be our private time?** *Inhale deeply... Exhale slowly...* **If unchecked, you'll one day come home to find all of your possessions boxed and stored to make way for the rest of her stuff, with the final touch of the dreaded bowl of potpourri.** *Inhale deeply... Exhale slowly...* **Yes my friend, you are in the middle of passive, aggressive hostile takeover in a struggle for power that you have no chance of winning.** *Tap ash into the ashtray...*

You've got to nip it in the bud early, always make sure that that toothbrush is swiftly returned to her overnight bag after use along with all the other crap she tries to leave behind. *Inhale deeply... Exhale slowly...* **Oh believe me, she will try to fight you on this, but you've got to be strong, a man's home is his castle. Pull up that drawbridge and arm the battlements as soon as she's crossed the moat.** *Inhale deeply... Exhale slowly...* **But it won't stop there, you may have won the battle but this age old war will continue to rage. You'll get a few warning shots across your bough in the form of unnecessary drama and mind games, but as my grandfather used to say 'If you gently rest your testicles in a sleeping lion's mouth and wedge your thumb up his arse, expect pain'.** *Tap ash into the ashtray...* **In other words don't leave yourself vulnerable if you're going on the offensive.** *Inhale deeply... Exhale slowly...* **Make no mistake, they are a cunning foe, even the strongest of us can be bested by a seductive smile or the promise of a shag, but it's a rookie mistake to think that the game isn't afoot.** *Inhale deeply... Exhale slowly...* **I've seen so many of my brothers in arms make complete twats of themselves in this battlefield we call love,** *Tap ash into the ashtray...* **obliviously giving in to a great cleavage as he flirts and squirms like he's fucking the hole in his trouser pocket.** *Inhale deeply... Exhale slowly...* **And so we don our black armbands for our fallen comrade as his Facebook status changes to 'In a Relationship'** *Inhale deeply... Exhale slowly...* **But oh so soon like a tortured ghost in the night come anguished phone calls and texts in the twilight hours 'Why is she doing this?' and 'What fresh female insanity is this?'** *Tap ash into the ashtray...* **And so we weep, for we know he is lost to us and we pray that he will find peace.**

Inhale deeply... Exhale slowly... **We find ourselves agonised in the knowledge that if he'd just wanked his brains out before engaging her in conversation, this turmoil could have been avoided.** *Inhale deeply... Exhale slowly...* **But then comes that fateful day as you sign into Facebook to see the status changed to 'Married' and you know he is dead to you in his servitude to her.** *Tap ash into the ashtray...* **Because the next time you see him, he seems confused, subdued and can't make a decision for himself. And you see the mortal dread in his eyes as you ask him if he'd like to meet up and he chokes before rushing off to call her to find out if it's okay.** *Inhale deeply... Exhale slowly...* **And you know deep inside that the battle is lost and your friend is beyond help. He's like the guy in the red top in Star Trek, as soon as he beams down, he's fucked.** *Inhale deeply... Exhale slowly...* **At least back in the old days they had the decency to hide the crazy and introduce it slowly so as not to scare you away, but alas, times have changed, these days they just expect you to accept it and strap in for the ride, and what a rollercoaster ride it is.** *Inhale deeply... Exhale slowly... Stub out in ashtray...* **For are we not all veterans and contestants in this game called love?**

Even more Stoned Thoughts
and Random Rambles...

Sometimes I dream of pressing a gun up under my chin, slowly squeezing the trigger and blowing the top of my head off in an explosion of blood, brains and skull fragment confetti, bursting out magnificently like fireworks and streamers... *Pull three papers from wrap...* I'm sure it would be very beautiful in its own way, a little macabre maybe but beautiful nonetheless... *Add bacci... Spread bacci...* And it's not because I want to die or that I am in any way suicidal, I'm just curious of what my last living thought will potentially be... *Strike lighter... Hold blim aloft...* I'd like to think it'll be something incredibly profound, something so deep as to touch me to tears, *Burn... Sprinkle liberally... Roll...* that maybe in that last second of life, all the secrets of the universe will be revealed to me as a whole, *Lick... Stick...* instead of glimpses beyond the veil in schizophrenic chimeras that promise so much more than they deliver... *Add roach... Put to lips... Light...* Besides, in reality it would probably be something simple like 'You fucking idiot, what a waste of a perfectly good afternoon', *Inhale deeply... Exhale slowly...* so I guess the price is a little too steep for something that will come naturally in time anyway... *Oh God YES, that hit the spot...* I mean you have to wonder at the brain's unyielding capacity for embracing illusions of self perception... *Inhale deeply... Exhale slowly...* And deep down, we know our illusions aren't real...

So we try to convince everyone around us, but even that is but another illusion in itself because all we are really trying to do is convince ourselves as we lay the groundwork *Inhale deeply... Exhale slowly...* and build our illusion's status to a whopping great delusion that keeps us sated as its bubble shields us from truths we would prefer not to face... *Tap ash into the ashtray...* But the problem with bubbles is they pop so easily and the fallout becomes toxic to our minds when the collateral damage is our sanity... *Inhale deeply... Exhale slowly...* Think about it, is that guy you see in the mirror each morning the same guy everyone else sees when you leave the house? Are you really flexing your pecs as you see him do or are you simply wiggling your moobs? *Inhale deeply... Exhale slowly...* There's no shame in it, denial is a powerful illusion, after all there are millions of comb over guys across the globe convinced you think they have hair... *Tap ash into the ashtray...* It's like writing, sometimes you are too close to the source to know if its any good until you get feedback... So when you do next look deeply into that mirror, you have to remember that you are probably the least qualified person to judge what you see there... *Inhale deeply... Exhale slowly...* You're too biased, so how can you possibly be neutral when you already have such strong preconceived judgements and opinions about the guy staring back at you? I mean, I know they say 'to thine own self be true' but I'm pretty sure that's impossible... *Inhale deeply... Exhale slowly...* We all have our secrets and we all have our demons that consume us from within, so all we can really do is try to move on and face them or we'll be forever running... *Tap ash into the ashtray...*

For if we dwell in the past, it will devour us, we'll be forever stuck there without a thought for the future, until eventually one day we find we are bitter, cynical old men wondering where our lives went... *Inhale deeply... Exhale slowly...* Just let it go... Unpack the baggage and fold it away tidily... Ding-Ding... The train has left Bitterville, next stop, Fresh Start City... LMAO!!! I know, I make it sound easy, but don't be fooled, its not... *Inhale deeply... Exhale slowly...* I'm a right one to talk, having sold my house on the corner of Denial Street in the quaint town of Delusionia, I moved to large apartment on Humility Avenue in Bitterville central... Sadly I'm having a little problem with shifting the property, so I'm stuck here until I can let it go and move on... *Tap ash into the ashtray...* Sweet, a metaphor wrapped in an analogy... Arr, smug mode... Bugger, I find myself stood atop Pride Hill as my body trembles in danger of being crushed under the weight of my swelling head... *Inhale deeply... Exhale slowly...* If you could kindly do me a favour and kick my legs out from under me, it would be much appreciated because pride always shines in prelude to a fall... I guess what I'm saying is just try to keep your illusions in check, enjoy them but don't let them own you... *Inhale deeply... Exhale slowly...* Keep a good grasp between fantasy and reality and remember that sometimes a smile is just a smile and that cute woman who beamed it did not mean 'Come take me Big Boy', she was simply greeting you good morning... *Tap ash into the ashtray...* Sure, enjoy the fantasy, take ten minutes out to yourself to whip out your penis and beat it to death as you conduct a solo symphony, after all, its the little things that make life worthwhile... *Inhale deeply... Exhale slowly...*

But the minute your toes curl and your knees buckle in that Halllelujah moment, zip up, shut up and get on with your day as you store that particular fantasy in the potential mastibatory material file in the storage space in your head... *Inhale deeply... Exhale slowly...* Just because she smiled at you, does not necessarily mean that you are going to be putting to her any time soon... After all, that's how lawsuits generally begin... *Tap ash into the ashtray...* Take me for example, people tell me I'm amazing, I'm a creative genius, I am a master of scribed darkness and I know that I should just accept the compliment humbly... *Inhale deeply... Exhale slowly...* But the reality is that I completely embraced it and my illusions have escalated to delusions of grandeur of such epic proportion... Oh yeah, believe me, in my head I picture myself on a huge throne overseeing my minions as they fight in arenas for my affections from their drab, grey little lives... *Inhale deeply... Exhale slowly...* A God who walks among his people... And I know I should keep it in check before it either gets out of hand or the bubble bursts but its such a wonderful place to be... And in hindsight, when I visited that sea food restaurant the other week, that waiter wasn't offering me sea kelp, he was telling me to 'Seek help'... *Inhale deeply... Exhale slowly... Stub out in ashtray...* Cheeky bastard, I should go back and smite him...

Mood Swings...

<u>Echoes in the Ghosts of Madness...</u>

Cleansing my soul
in a baptism of fire,
burning in the darkness
that seeps through breaches
of fractured quintessence...

Folding to voices
that endlessly cry out
from the empty shadows,
such elusive eidolon
that call beyond the veil...

Manipulating my reality
in distortions of perception,
built on foundations
of falsehood,
holding back the storm,
suppressing a fury
that erodes the stones
of all I hold in axiom...

...Forever seeking cessation
for my fading Élan vital...

__Fighting my Nature...__

My mind and body
in conflict,
one refusing
to acknowledge
what the other
so desperately needs,
a battle of wills
whose casualty is sanity…

The mind so sure
that love is unnecessary,
a temporary
hormonal imbalance
that drains finances
and distracts
from the greater
creative endeavors
that secure an illusion
of immortality…

The body, yearning,
primal in its needs,
unrelenting in its craving
to be touched, to feel,
to have, to hold,
beating the passion
of a poet's heart,
programmed
at the cellular level
before life began
as the mind
seeks to reboot
the system…

This war of body
and mind
that wearies the soul
in the battle waged
for dominancy
and supremacy
of will, restraint
and ideological victory
over human nature
versus
disciplined thought
in a temperance
of emotion...

But alas, it saddens me,
for there will be no victory
for either side,
tainting my soul
as my mind
stands to lose
its last vestiges
of passion
and humanity,
as my body loses
its ability to
connect with others,
a bitter irony
that either victory
will be hollow in its loss...

...I am so very tired of fighting my nature...
...Its breaking my heart...
...Its killing me...

...I have to end this...

...The Demon is Awake...

The Demon is awake...
No more do I suppress him...
Oh no, his time has come
as he knew it would
and I embrace him
with open arms...

He intoxicates my mind,
burns his mark
upon my soul
in visions
of the chaos
he will bring
in my name...

He is the master manipulator,
the long game player,
the bringer of the storm
and you are exposed
before his eyes...

Such words of fatal truth
that push to press
the axiom bomb
that detonates
the maxim's toxicity,
exploding the shroud
of falsehoods,
beheld in the book
of stratagem...

For the pawns are rife
in the trinity of mind wars
and your games
of validation
become the
Demon's
playground…

You will see
how creative
this genius can be
as the Demon
tears your world apart,
brick by brick,
layer by layer
in subliminal ideas,
stray thoughts
and metaphoric rage
in divine retribution…

You won't even know
the game is afoot,
but you can stop this…
The truth will set you free…

But alas, this is not who I am
or who I would wish to be,
the Demon is back
in his box
so be thankful
I am not a vengeful God…

…But…

…Beware the path you walk…

All That I Become...

So much that I would wish to do,
but days just pass to weeks,
and time is such a cruel mistress,
for king of all the freaks.

Weeks that pass to months and years,
my soul it grows so cold,
empty, hollow, growing numb
as voices grow so bold

Visions in the quiet time
that bid me scribe their tales,
seeing through illusion's eyes
as madness soon prevails.

I walk unseen by all around,
I live like I am dead,
a ghost who walks a lonely path
and lives inside my head.

So much that I would wish from life,
a reason to survive,
if I could hear my heart but once,
to know I'm still alive.

But I know it's not my fate,
I walk in endless night,
balancing a path between
the darkness and the light.

Always seeking who I was
to guide who I become,
holding back a demon's wrath,
ensure I don't succumb.

Please remember who I am
and all I have achieved,
wrapped in my cocoon of lies
of dreams that I believed.

My words shall live beyond my time,
please cherish all they say,
for they define the man I am
in life and death's ballet.

Waiting...

Always stood at the crossroads of life,
choices to be made,
left or right?
Darkness? Light?
Or maybe the grey
that flows between...

Sell my soul
or just have it crushed?
So many choices,
so little time, so much to do...

Yet still I stand,
unsure of the path I walk,
waiting for a sign
to lead me onward,
waiting for my life to begin...

Did I miss it?
Would be just my luck... BUGGER!!!

<u>Nevermore...</u>

Behold me, for I am broken,
my heart so cold,
lifeless where once beat
the passion of a supernova soul,
an event horizon that collapses
and guides me on a destructive path
to temperance in the ashes of love…

No longer do I sing my adoration
in soothing lullabies
that drive the demons
from my mind,
haunted by the hand of fate,
no longer do I feel
the yearning of divine adulation,
nor crave the dreams of what could be…

So lost, so alone
in the world once more,
dying in the light,
embracing the darkness
as the sands of time
slip through my open fingers,
trod to dust in the long cold embers
of the endless twilight Winter,
bitter in the discontented cries
of all that I have become…

…all that I have lost…
So numb, so empty,
the hollow man cries out to love…

"…Bequeath me nevermore…"

<u>Tell Me How...</u>

How can you tell them
you love them
when your heart feels
like it's been shredded
through a corybantic
cheese grater
and spread liberally
over a phrenetic Bolognese?

When your insides
have been allegorically
scooped out with a blunt,
rusty potato knife
and force fed back to you,
leaving you hollow and empty
as pain shifts to numbness
and all you feel is cold
as paralysis creeps
like a cranial sniper,
taking its shot
in the assassination
of your fading acumen?

Drifting like a ghost
because life
is for the living...

...So again I ask, how can you tell them?

Cause and Effect...

Today, tomorrow's yesterday,
all the things that we would say
as our souls are led astray
in the most impossible way...

You know, we really are afraid
of the choices we've all made,
in the lives that we all trade
as our morals start to fade...

And so, it is really up to you,
all the things you choose to do,
all the lies that you pursue
in the depths that you sink too...

You know, we are never truly free,
to be who we want to be,
with so much we'd like to see
to define ourselves as me...

And so, in the darkness now we fall,
with no one to hear us call,
round our hearts we build a wall
from a world where we're so small...

For now, in the lives that we all lead
in a world that preaches greed,
as the darkness starts to feed
on the virtues we all bleed...

For us, it's so easy to pretend,
that our souls will all transcend,
that our lives will find an end
in misdeeds that we amend...

And we, could be living out our days
in the glory that we blaze,
in the changing of our ways,
just to ease our soul's malaise…

In life, there is never selfless deed,
just an act to fulfil need,
to appease our shame's concede
of a conscience that we heed…

And so, there is always consequence
to the actions we dispense,
to our heart there's no defence
when we strike on the offence…

For some, they will charge through life in pride,
for they dare not look inside,
for their truth and lies collide
as their loyalties divide…

In life, there's a balance we must make,
of the things we give and take,
of the things we must forsake
or our grounding starts to quake…

And now, there is not much more to say,
so just don't be led astray
as you live from day to day
or you'll hate what you portray…

You know, that we all know right from wrong
and that life is but a song,
so we really must be strong
if we all want to belong…

And so, as I bid you all goodbye,
question all that you deny,
for in life you can but try
to find peace before you die…

Fractured...

Silence falls,
as loud as rapturous applause,
deafening me in the emptiness,
a chasm that echoes
in the thoughts and obsessions
that trace lineage in acts
that are so
very far from proud...

Overwhelmed
in such blind saturninity,
despondently numb
to the accusatory stares,
bequeathed
in catatonic secrets,
best left hushed
in shallow graves
that beg to be unearthed...

Bitterness bites
in acrimony of self loathing,
ravaging my soul's malaise
in contempt of justice's folly,
and so tears fall
like rain to the storm
as thunder gives way to rage,
for none shall find shelter
from its unspent fury...

Streams of consciousness
screech to oceans of sorrow,
turbulent as waves of regret
crash shores of madness,
dragged on currents
of the past,
pulled to depths of despair,
beyond the truths we create
to ease the burden
of our guilty hearts...

Can't breathe, can't see,
can't hold on...
Delusions fracture,
shattering in the light of truth
as falsehoods burn
in the rising dawn
of axiom's promise,
paving paths to hindsight
in the cold light of day...

...What have I done?

Flames of Sagacity...

He burns in the flames
of his own sagacity,
clawing his way back
from the abyss
of potential futurities,
and so he is beheld
on the threshold of madness,
a king who humbles
to the darkness,
embracing his demons
in communion
of the worlds he creates,
scribing in the shadows
of perception,
appeasing the voices
that call from echoes
of shifting beliefs,
grasping for dreams
of normality
in a maelstrom
of nightmares...

...patiently he waits,
crushed in the event horizon,
decaying in the collapse
of his supernova soul,
burning brightly,
drawn into
the ebb and flow
of his broken mind...

Lost...

I walk in so many worlds,
defined in mirrors of perception,
defying actuality yet bound
to laws of physicality
as paths diverge
in the choices made…

I float through
an ocean of dreams,
pulled on currents
of subconscious descent,
drowning in waves
of memory,
beheld in
turbulent storms
of unspent rage,
sinking to such
gelid depths,
rewriting the traumas
of the past…

I fly in chimera skies ,
a God to the worlds I create,
cleansed in a rain
of sagacity,
seeking meaning
in the gifts
that I'm bestowed,
embracing my own
separate reality…

I am so very, very lost…

I'm not gonna crack...

I like it, feelings numb to bliss,
my mind is lost to the abyss,
my heart is craving Reaper's kiss,
my soul is dead to all of this.

I miss you, couldn't tell you why,
I want you, time has gone to try.
Where were you, they wanted me to die?
I try too, my hands just won't comply.

I love you, I never tell you so,
I need you, I thought you'd like to know.
I'm leaving, a gift that I bestow,
it's hard to know when to let go.

I kill you, driving me insane,
I feel you, my mind it brings me pain,
in my life, there's little left to gain,
of my thoughts, there's nothing to retain.

…But I'm not gonna crack…

This piece was inspired by the song 'Lithium' by Nirvana

Beneath...

Beneath the masks we wear,
insecurities writhe
in the murky depths of self doubt,
hiding away from a world
of expectation,
craving acceptance
in the roles we play,
seeking validation
in the acts we perform...

Beneath the walls we build,
our hearts grow cold,
emotion stymied
in suppression
as the light fades,
casting our souls
to the darkness
as brick by brick
and stone by stone,
the blockade
grows ever higher,
burying us alive
as prisoners in our minds...

Beneath the flesh we wear,
we weary to the passing ages,
resentful that we live to die,
our lifetimes, but a fleeting moment,
blinked in the eye of eternity,
a breath on the winds of time,
sighed in acceptance
of a fate that binds us to causality...

Dying from the time we are born...

www.ingramcontent.com/pod-product-compliance
Lightning Source LLC
LaVergne TN
LVHW011352080426
835511LV00005B/261